IT AIN'T PRETTY
BUT IT'S REAL

by
John Drummond

CHICAGO SPECTRUM PRESS
LOUISVILLE, KENTUCKY 40207

CHICAGO SPECTRUM PRESS
4824 BROWNSBORO CENTER
LOUISVILLE, KENTUCKY 40207

Printed in the U.S.A.

10 9 8 7 6 5 4 3 2 1

ISBN: 978-1-58374-175-7

Cover photo by Arthur Caudy
Caudy's pals are depicting a mob chieftain being arrested by
the authorities.
Left to right: Ken Tatarelis (holding Boom mike)
    John Drummond (holding Channel 2 mike)
    Hank Stanic
    Bill Horn (in handcuffs)
    Jim Smith
    Larry Orpic (in uniform)
    Bob Sadler (in jacket)
    Roth Mui (with camera)

To my parents Frank and Maude Drummond,
who did so much for me.

ACKNOWLEDGMENTS

A number of people were most helpful to me in preparing this book.

As was the case in my earlier effort, *Thirty Years In The Trenches*, Arthur Caudy drew the short straw and had the tedious job of scanning a large number of pictures and transferring them to CDs.

Ed Marshall, a crackerjack producer at Channel Two, had the unenviable task of obtaining photos of subjects long gone from the scene.

Deborah Segal, a Channel Two archivist and a good one, was willing to help search the WBBM-TV library for tapes of individuals who are featured in the book. That was no easy assignment.

I also want to thank Rick Kramer, digital assets manager at Channel Two, for his role in transferring a number of videotapes to discs.

And thanks to the many Channel Two cameramen and camerawomen, past and present, who tried so hard to make news personalities smile for the birdie. And let's not forget the Channel Two "Brass" for allowing me to use WBBM-TV newstape as video for illustrations in this book.

The same holds true to their video colleagues at WHO-TV in Des Moines and WREX-TV in Rockford.

Kudos also go to my son Duncan for his help in editing the work.

And last, but not least, thanks to Dorothy Kavka of Evanston Publishing, a member of the grammar police and a professor of comas, question marks, quotations, and periods.

INTRODUCTION

Here we go again. After our first book *Thirty Years In The Trenches* was published in the late 1990s, it dawned on us that we had left out a number of stories that were good yarns. So back to work we went in order to have a rematch.

We've entitled this effort *It Ain't Pretty But It's Real*. That title might ring a bell for some of our readers because that was the slogan in the 1970s for WBBM-TV newscasts. Those newscasts, by the way, attracted a large number of viewers and helped ring the cash register at Channel Two.

Again, like their predecessors, most of these stories, but not all, deal with Chicago area locales or Chicago area personalities. However, I feel that readers who have no Chicago connection will also enjoy these pieces.

Being something of a packrat, I've kept hundreds of scripts, audio tapes, government documents, transcripts, and clippings of stories with which I have had more than a passing interest. We've updated some of these stories by doing recent interviews with newsmakers and sources. With the exception of the Bradley sisters' disappearance and the Killer Poet segment, I personally covered all of the stories in this book either for Channel Two in Chicago or WHO in Des Moines, Iowa.

There are more pieces about hard boiled criminals and the Chicago Outfit here than in our last effort although there are still a number of chapters on characters that will ring a bell with many readers. As we said in our earlier book, you won't read about these stories in the Chicago guide books or travel brochures. The same holds true once again.

CONTENTS

1

THE MISSING POLICEMAN

I can't think of any other story that I covered that was more puzzling, and yet as tragic, than that of the missing policeman.

Patrolman Anthony Raymond, kidnapped by robbers. Hillside P.D. photo.

On the evening of October 1, 1972, a young suburban Hillside police officer pulled a car over on the westbound ramp of the Eisenhower Expressway at Mannheim Road. It appeared on the surface to be a routine traffic stop, but it ended in the death of the policeman. The officer was 25 year old Anthony Raymond, married, and the father of two small children.

Raymond was last heard from when he radioed his dispatcher saying something like this, "This is car 406, I don't like the way this looks." Before Raymond could finish his message he was cut off by another suburban police department operating on the same radio band. At that time in 1972, some 17 suburban police departments were using the same frequency. Authorities believe that Raymond had started to give the license plate number of the suspicious car transmitting the words "Double L five."

There was one witness. A youth, who attended a local high school, claimed he saw a man holding what he thought was a pistol on a uniformed cop at about 10:12 P.M. That's near the time that Raymond had radioed the Hillside department. The teenager added that Raymond and the suspect were standing near a car, which he believed was a wine colored Cadillac Coup de Ville.

About two and a half to three minutes after Raymond's radio call, another squad car arrived on the scene. According to the officer, he found Raymond's squad car with the lights flashing and the doors open, but he could find no trace of Officer Raymond.

Raymond did not know that shortly before he pulled the suspicious car over that there had been a robbery by three masked men at the nearby Swedish Manor restaurant in Hillside. The restaurant was about a quarter mile away from the spot where Raymond confronted the men. Investigators soon correctly theorized that there was a connection between the $5,000 restaurant robbery and the disappearance and presumed abduction of the Hillside officer. Hillside police believed that Raymond was not shot on the spot by the robbers and that there was a good chance that he was still alive.

The Raymond case touched off several searches including one where some thirty Cook County Sheriff's policemen and other law enforcement officers, accompanied by dogs, combed forest preserves and other areas for the missing cop. Helicopters from the Sheriff's Department and Illinois State Police conducted an aerial search of the area hoping that Raymond might be tied up and dumped in a remote location by the kidnapers.

A $1,000 reward was offered by a bank in Hillside for the arrest and conviction of the men who abducted the police officer, but it brought in no meaningful leads.

Then several days after Raymond disappeared, the police thought they had gotten a break in the case. A woman who lived in Grundy County, near Coal City, which is southwest of Chicago, told authorities that she saw a man stumbling along the bank of the Mazon River. The man had dark trousers with a stripe on the side, similar to many police uniforms. A neighbor of the woman said that she later heard a bump on the door which lawmen interpreted to mean that Raymond or somebody was trying to get in.

The Coal City woman was then shown a photograph of Raymond which she tentatively identified as the man she saw stumbling along the river bank.

Then on top of that, a farmer told police that he saw a man staggering along Illinois Highway 113 which is near the Mazon River. Later a bloody handkerchief was found beside the road.

The three "sightings" led to a massive search party, the largest I'd ever seen. Some 400 lawmen and volunteers plus assorted news personnel swarmed into the area in the early morning hours of a beautiful fall day. The searchers, at arms' length from each other, marched through corn and soybean fields, as well as wooded areas. Bloodhounds were used in the effort as helicopters swept over the region in a futile attempt to find Raymond. The search went on for two days and it was very thorough. But nothing turned up as far as Raymond was concerned. Authorities never did find out who the mysterious man was who was seen staggering along the river bank. The lawmen, obviously disappointed at the outcome, felt justified in the effort saying, "We had to give it a shot."

For the Raymond family it was a bitter disappointment. They were hoping against hope that it was Anthony who residents had seen near Coal City. Even a boost in the reward money to more than $8,000 failed to produce any viable leads. The question as to whether Anthony was alive or dead continued to plague the family.

I visited the Raymond family, along with a WBBM-TV film crew, shortly after the young officer had disappeared. It was a very sad scene. Raymond's two young sons, four year old Anthony, Jr. and three year old Michael, recited a prayer for the safe return of their father. And the youngsters' mother, Margaret Raymond, made a tearful appeal to the kidnapers or those with knowledge of the abduction to come forward and tell the authorities what had happened.

Unfortunately the case grew cold and as fall turned to winter what leads the police had began to dry up. It seemed that the mystery of the missing policemen would not be solved. More than 700 persons and some two thousand leads were checked out by Cook County Sheriff's Police and Hillside Police in the months following the abduction. An FBI bulletin described the 25 year old officer as well as pointing out that he had a gun, his two way radio, and handcuffs. Sgt. Frank Grossman, in an interview with the *Chicago Tribune*, said, "We can find no parallel where a policeman has been abducted without being found."

Policeman from Hillside, who worked long hours trying to find their fellow officer, turned their overtime pay to Mrs. Raymond. The public too was touched by the tragedy with some citizens offering to donate money to the family.

Then several truck drivers came forward and told investigators that they saw a car similar to the one believed used in the kidnapping being loaded into a semi-trailer truck in south suburban Summit. The truck drivers said the auto was a burgundy colored GM vehicle although they couldn't be sure if it was a Cadillac. The car, they told police, had been stripped of its license plates. The reader will recall that a youth told detectives that he saw Raymond being held at gunpoint by a man standing by what the teenager described as a wine colored Cadillac Coup de Ville. Lawmen theorized that the kidnapers, fearing that the Cadillac used in the restaurant robbery was too hot to drive around in anymore, decided to dispose of it.

For ten months it appeared that investigators were getting nowhere in the Raymond case. However, in reality, detectives, by the summer of 1973, had a pretty good idea who the culprits were and what had happened to the missing policeman. At least two informants in the parlance of the underworld had "dropped a dime." One of those was Robert Harder, a former confederate of the kidnapers. Harder and another man, Vincent McCabe, provided information to police agencies that led to the discovery of Raymond's body and the arrests of Silas Fletcher and Robert Martinez.

Silas Fletcher
Convicted of killing Officer Raymond

Ironically, Harder was found murdered, shot in the face, in a farm field near Dwight, Illinois, several months before Fletcher went on trial. Despite Harder's demise, the damage was done. He had provided detectives what they wanted to know.

A second man believed involved in the Raymond caper was Jesse Millard of Schaumburg, but his case was settled out of court. Millard was killed during the holdup of a coin shop in Winchester, Indiana, a small community near the Ohio state line. His partner in that ill fated robbery attempt was the aforementioned Silas Fletcher.

The coin shop heist turned out to be no easy score for Fletcher and Millard. Millard was killed by the wife of the coin shop owner who, during the robbery, ran upstairs to the second floor, called police and grabbed a revolver. She then turned the gun on Millard and fatally shot the intruder.

According to the police report, while Fletcher was pistol whipping a store employee, the owner of the shop got a hold of his shotgun and pointed it at Fletcher. Silas, police said, wisely surrendered and was bundled off to the Randolph County Jail. A third man involved in the robbery fled the scene.

Acting on informant information the third man involved in the Raymond abduction, Robert Martinez was arrested in Las Vegas and later brought back to Chicago to face the music.

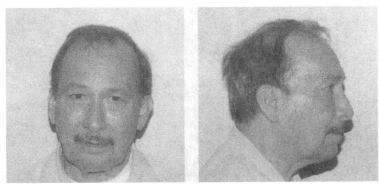

Robert Martinez
Fletcher's accomplice in the killing.

Authorities were told that Raymond's body was buried at an abandoned farm about ten miles southeast of Rhinelander, Wisconsin. The farm located in Onieda County, was at one time owned by Fletcher's sister and her former husband. It was an area that Silas knew well since he grew up in Oneida County before moving to Chicago.

A contingent of Wisconsin and Illinois lawmen descended on the property in August of 1973, some ten months after the policeman had disappeared. The police were told the body was on the property but the informant couldn't pinpoint the exact location. It was no easy task to find the grave since searchers were confronted by stretches of pine and birch trees all over the property. Aerial searches were conducted, but authorities found the grave the old fashioned way by "hoofing" around the farm.

One lawman noticed the vegetation in one spot was different than that of the surrounding area. The color of the grass was different too. Some readers may recall that a similar situation led to the discovery of the Spilotro brothers' grave near Morocco, Indiana, in 1986.

The lawmen began digging and before long they made their grisly discovery. Raymond's body was found with his wrists handcuffed behind him. He was in his Hillside Police uniform and his star and name plate were still pinned to his chest. However, his gun and holster were missing. The body, considering that Raymond had been dead for ten months, was not badly decomposed. Authorities said because the missing man had been buried in firm soil rather than in swampy or marsh land, the body was fairly well preserved. The autopsy, conducted in Madison, revealed that Raymond had been strangled and stabbed.

About two months after Raymond's body was located the body of a young woman was found in a grave some 150 feet away from where Raymond had been buried. It turned out the remains were that of one Sarah Hamilton of Forest Park who Wisconsin authorities said was the victim of a botched abortion. It was hard to determine how long the young woman had been dead since her body was badly decomposed, but her parents never saw her alive again after she left home in 1970, an 18 year old graduate of Proviso East High School.

An informant later told detectives that Sarah Hamilton had paid $1,200 for an abortion that was performed at a Chicago hotel. According to the informant the operation proved fatal to Sarah. Detectives said that Silas Fletcher at one time was the head of an abortion ring that included fellow defendant Robert Martinez and the late Jesse Millard.

Meanwhile, investigators under the command of Cook County Sheriff's Police Officer Richard Quagliano, were building their case against Fletcher who had been extradited from Indiana so he could face murder and kidnapping charges in Illinois. Police had received information from two informants that Fletcher was responsible for the murder.

According to the detectives' scenario Raymond, after being abducted near the expressway, was driven to Fletcher's home in suburban Hanover Park There in Fletcher's garage the young policeman was strangled and stabbed four times. Raymond then bled to death and was stuffed into a 55 gallon steel drum and taken in a jeep to northern Wisconsin where he was buried.

Prosecutors James Meltreger, Daniel Wolff, and Ronald Neville built a solid case although their evidence was largely circumstantial. One of the highlights for the prosecution came when Fletcher's former brother-in-law James Ehmann testified that he saw the defendant washing blood out of the inside of his jeep the morning after Raymond had been abducted in Hillside.

The state also scored points when Fletcher's brother Douglas told the jury that Silas had asked him to help bury a body on the farm in November or early December, 1970. The state was trying to show the jury that Fletcher had used the Oneida County property as a burial site before he had disposed of Raymond's body

Fletcher's sister Marianne also testified implicating Silas in the Raymond disappearance.

Fletcher didn't go down without a fight. He took the stand contending he was out hunting alone in Wisconsin between September 28th and October 2nd.

It didn't help the defense's case when that high school youth told the jury that he had seen a man resembling Fletcher talking to Raymond on the expressway ramp moments before the police officer disappeared.

Prosecutors, as we mentioned before, had mainly a circumstantial case against Silas but the jury went with it and after a little more than four hours of deliberation found Fletcher guilty of murder and aggravated kidnapping.

As the Fletcher trial was winding down in November of 1974, his cohort Robert Martinez lost his extradition battle in Nevada, where he was being held on marijuana charges, and was brought back to Chicago.

Martinez was put on trial a year later in the fall of 1975. This time the state produced its star witness Vincent McCabe, who prosecutors felt wasn't needed in the first trial. The 37 year old McCabe a onetime bookmaking partner of Martinez, was described by prosecutors as Martinez's best friend, and McCabe had quite a tale to tell to the jury of eight men and four women.

According to McCabe, Martinez told him the whole story about the abduction and death of Raymond. He also had to tell the jury about two fibs he had committed back in 1973 when he was called before a grand jury investigating the Raymond case. Yes, he lied then, McCabe admitted, but that was to protect his onetime pal Martinez. Now McCabe claimed he was telling the whole truth and nothing but the truth.

Then in gripping detail McCabe testified about the last moments in Officer Raymond's life. This is what Martinez, the state's star witness, told the jury.

According to McCabe, Raymond pleaded for his life after Martinez, Fletcher, and Millard had abducted the policeman shortly after the restaurant robbery. McCabe said Martinez told him Raymond was forced at gun point into the robber's car and then handcuffed. Raymond reportedly said to his kidnapers, "Why are you taking me? What did I do? What's wrong?" Later the policeman allegedly told the three men, "I've got a wife and two kids."

Those pleas fell on deaf ears although McCabe testified that Martinez and the two others promised not to kill Raymond. Apparently they were trying to calm Raymond down until they got to their destination, Fletcher's garage in Hanover Park. Once they arrived at Fletcher's property, McCabe explained, they blindfolded and strangled him. Fletcher reportedly stabbed Raymond in the back saying, "I'll give him the coup de grace."

McCabe's testimony was pretty strong stuff and it was a major factor in convincing the jury to return a guilty verdict in November of 1975.

Earlier in the year Judge Richard Fitzgerald sentenced the boss of the operation, Silas Fletcher to a 100 to 200 year prison term. The diminutive Martinez, he's five foot five, didn't fare much better. He received a 75 to 150 year stretch in the penitentiary. Judge Fitzgerald said he sentenced Martinez to a shorter prison term because he felt the evidence showed that Fletcher was the ringleader.

Attorney Jim Meltreger, one of the prosecutors in the case, remembers Silas Fletcher to this day. Meltreger, now in private practice, told me recently that "Fletcher was one of the meanest guys we [he and fellow prosecutors] ever encountered." Meltreger said Fletcher was a short stocky guy with strong hands. Meltreger recalled, "He was cold as cold could be."

Both Fletcher and Martinez, now in their early 70s, were incarcerated at last report at the Dixon Correctional Facility in north central Illinois.

Ironically the death of Anthony Raymond spurred many suburban police departments to upgrade their radio equipment. Some Hillside police officers have long contended that

Raymond would be alive today if his radio hadn't failed him. They argue that if they had gotten the license plate, they could have been on the lookout for the Cadillac or even gone to Fletcher's Hanover Park home where the murder took place.

At the time of Raymond's murder many police departments were sharing a single channel. That's not the case today as more sophisticated communications equipment is being used by law enforcement agencies.

But for Anthony's widow Margaret the new equipment was little solace. It wouldn't bring her husband back. The family continued to be haunted by the affair. Only five years after Martinez was convicted, Margaret Raymond died, a young woman heartbroken over the loss of her husband.

2

A TOUGH OLD BIRD

He was 70 years old, but here was Silas Jayne battling with Circuit Court bailiffs as he was being led from a Daley Center elevator to a courtroom. The bailiffs were trying to put handcuffs on Si, but the septuagenarian would have no part of it. That led to a shoving match and words were exchanged. Chief Bailiff Edward Kacmarek said Jayne had

Silas Jayne, struggling. Silas had a bad temper. WBBM-TV photo.

threatened to beat the heck out of him and two other bailiffs as they marched Jayne to the courtroom.

I witnessed that scuffle back in 1978, along with several other reporters and camera crews. Although Jayne was angry, I had a sneaking suspicion that he was putting on a show for the media. Si was as crazy as a fox. He was well aware that cameras were present and he wanted the public to see on television an old man fighting off three or four men half his age.

Despite his track record, Si didn't come across as the Devil Incarnate. He was a rough hewn type, plain spoken, even jovial at times, and when in the mood could put on quite a charm act. I interviewed Jayne on several occasions and he could come across like a favorite uncle.

But there was a dark side to Jayne. He was ruthless, no doubt about it. And you didn't want to cross him. Even Nick Guido, a notorious home invader and a cellmate of Si, reportedly was deathly afraid of him.

Jayne was an unscrupulous horse trader who wouldn't think twice about torching a rival's barn full of horses. He was convicted of a murder conspiracy to kill his younger brother in a modern day Cain and Abel rivalry. However, Jayne knew horse flesh, there was no doubt about that. He always took pride in discussing the horses he was raising and showing. But it was also buyer beware. He bought and sold horses, sometimes peddling a glue factory nag at an inflated price. His clients on the show horse circuit were the silk stocking type, wealthy business executives whose daughter or niece wanted to become a skilled equestrian. Granted Jayne sometimes bilked his customers out of big bucks but at the same time his horses garnered their share of blue ribbons and so did his clients.

Silas Jayne was born on July 3, 1907, too young to have served in World War I and too old for World War II. Si wouldn't have been eligible for military service anyway since he was convicted at the age of 17 of rape. A convicted felon, Jayne served a year in a reformatory before getting into the business of training and showing horses on a full time basis.

Jayne grew up with a pack of siblings. He was the eldest son in a family of eight girls and four boys When Si and the rest of the clan were young, his parents separated. He was brought up by his mother and a Waukegan lawyer by the name of George Spunner.

Si was followed by his younger brothers DeForest, Frank, and then George. George, who later became Silas's bitterest rival, was born in 1923 when Si was already 16 years old. From the start the boys were excellent horsemen. Soon they were hanging around and working at Chicago area stables.

By the early 1930s the boys were known as "the Jayne gang" when they brought wild horses from the west to what was then a railhead in Woodstock, Illinois. Like shades of a Buck Jones movie, the Jayne boys would drive a herd of horses through the streets of Woodstock before the amazed citizenry.

Silas Jayne with one of his horses. WBBM-TV photo.

They soon had the reputation of tough drinking cowboys who played as hard as they worked.

DeForest Jayne may have been the most skilled horseman of the group, but in 1938, "D" as he was called by his friends, shot himself with a 12 gauge shotgun several days after his fiancée committed suicide. After DeForest's death Si claimed he became a mentor to his younger brother George.

By 1940 Si had his own riding academy in suburban River Grove. It was called Green Tree Stables and it was there that a fire of undetermined origin killed ten of Jayne's horses. That was the first of a series of suspicious fires that occurred at a stable owned by the Jaynes or at one of their competitor's facilities.

In the 1950s George Jayne had gone into the stable business himself and soon was emerging as a rival to his older brother. George's horses were not only going head to head with Si's entries, but were often coming out on top. In one incident, at the Lake Forest horse show at Onwentsia, a bay mare owned by George won the open jumping event. Si reportedly was enraged and according to George's daughter, Linda, Si was overheard telling George, "I'll kill you, you S. O. B." Around that time, authorities say, several unsuccessful attempts were made on George's life. That set the stage for an event that put the Jayne feud on the front pages.

On June 14, 1965, a champion equestrian by the name of Cheryl Lynn Rude was killed at the Tri-Color Stables in unincorporated Palatine. The 22 year old Rude died when she turned on the ignition of George Jayne's Cadillac. Within seconds the car exploded. Three sticks of dynamite which had been placed under the hood detonated ripping the auto to shreds. Rude died instantly, an innocent victim of the feud between Silas and George.

Authorities were convinced that George was the intended victim and that Rude was accidentally killed when George asked her to move his car so workmen could finish painting a nearby barn. Although investigators believed that the bomber did his dastardly deed at the behest of Silas Jayne, nothing came of it for years.

In 1997, 32 years after the bombing and 10 years after Silas had died, an arrest was made. The bomber, according to police, was James Blottiaux, a truck driver from the south side. Blottiaux's name had surfaced during the initial stages of the investigation but nothing had come from it. However, years later, after investigators were looking into some cases of arson and insurance fraud in the horse industry, the Rude case again became a priority item.

Blottiaux was put on trial and, with the testimony of an accomplice who was given immunity, the 56 year old south sider was convicted. Blottiaux contended it was the accomplice, a used car salesman, and not he who was the bomber. The jury didn't buy it and Blottiaux was found guilty. Prosecutors said that Blottiaux had even boasted to others that he had killed Rude and that the cops would never pin it on him. It was never proven but authorities are convinced that Blottiaux was paid ten thousand dollars to kill George Jayne, but the plot went awry when Cheryl Rude started George's car and was blown to smithereens. Blottiaux had worked as a handy man at one of Silas's stables.

James Blottiaux, who professed his innocence at sentencing, was given a 100 to 300 year jail term by Judge Michael Toomin. At last report he was serving his sentence at the Menard Maximum Security Prison in downstate Chester, Illinois.

After Rude's murder George Jayne needed no warnings from his friends that Silas was out to kill him. One friend reportedly told George that he ought to hire a hit man to have Silas taken out. At any rate an ex-convict by the name of Frank Michelle Jr. entered the picture. According to associates of George Jayne, Michelle went to Silas's farm near Elgin one night to install a new transmitter on Silas's car. The old transmitter had malfunctioned. The younger Jayne wanted the device on his brother's vehicle to beep whenever Silas's car was near. That way George would know if Silas was in the neighborhood.

That's one version of the story. Silas told it differently. Silas claimed he answered the doorbell on a snowy winter night in January of 1969, only to hear two shots which crashed through the door. The elder Jayne says he retaliated, firing a number of rounds from a window overlooking the front yard which was lit up. One of the shots hit home, wounding Michelle. Si then grabbed an M-I Army carbine and finished Michelle off.

Silas Jayne said the man was sent to kill him and he claimed to have found George Jayne's phone and address in the intruder's pocket. Silas said he also found a map on the dead man showing where the older Jayne lived. Silas Jayne was never charged in the Michelle shooting. He always contended he acted in self defense.

The gloves were now off and the next saga in the Jayne brother's feud ended with the death of George in a spectacular shooting incident. By 1970 Silas was frantically issuing contracts on his brother's life. Si had tried to kill his younger brother before. There was the Cheryl Rude incident and shortly after that Si had allegedly hired two men to take care of George. That backfired and in 1966 Silas went on trial for conspiracy to commit murder. The case fell apart and Jayne walked.

Si then put on a full court press trying to find someone capable of killing his younger brother. He literally scoured the bushes in an attempt to locate what he considered a good man, one with the guts and ability to carry out the grisly assignment.

With money to burn it didn't take Si long to find a taker. Edward Nefeld, then Chief of Detectives at the Markham Police Department, was on Jayne's payroll and the south suburban cop felt he found a willing recruit in Melvin Adams, a one time dishwasher. Nefeld instructed Adams to contact Joseph LaPlaca, a handyman for Silas. LaPlaca told Adams that Jayne had a job for him.

An appointment was set up for Silas, LaPlaca, and Adams to meet in Jayne's Cadillac outside a restaurant in Kane County near Elgin. It was at this meeting, according to Adams, that Jayne offered him a contract to kill Silas's younger brother. Adams, who would become the state's key witness in the murder trial, said Jayne agreed to pay him $30,000 to kill George.

Silas told Adams that he had been trying to kill his younger brother for ten years and he warned Adams that if George's wife Marion or their children got in the way, they would also have to be killed. Adams claimed Si first suggested machine gunning George on the expressway. But Adams said he told Jayne he was against the idea. Then Si allegedly told Adams, "If you can get him alive, put him in the trunk of your car and we'll bury him on the farm."

Adams and Si's handyman, Joseph LaPlaca followed George to several horse shows in San Antonio and New Orleans, but despite several opportunities, Adams failed to even attempt to shoot Si's brother.

Adams was a neophyte hit man. He had never killed anyone in his life and was obviously not the man to pull the trigger. So, Adams not willing to give up his lucrative fee, sub-contracted the job to a fellow worker. That man was Julius Barnes who had held several jobs on the south side, including a stint in a glue factory. Barnes was to get $12,500 for the assignment while Adams kept the rest of the 30 grand for himself.

Adams would later testify that he and Barnes checked out George Jayne's home in northwest suburban Inverness a number of times before deciding to kill their victim at his house. During their surveillance of the Jayne household Barnes recommended the use of a high powered rifle. Adams, with the aid of his wife, obtained a 30.06 rifle from a south suburban policeman on the pretense of using it on a hunting trip.

The killers picked the night of October 28, 1970, to carry out their scheme. Adams who was given immunity in the case testified that he parked his car, a 1969 Ford, near George Jayne's home. The men raised the hood of the vehicle in order to avoid suspicion. Showing no emotion when he was on the stand, Adams said Barnes got out of the car, armed with the high powered rifle, and said, "I'm going to take a look."

Adams told the packed courtroom that he watched Barnes outlined against a basement window. Then he said the murder weapon was raised several times, then there was a "flash and an explosion. Julius came back to me and told me he got Jayne." Adams quoted Barnes as saying "I kept trying to get a bead on him, but the old lady, Mrs. Jayne, kept getting in the way. But I got him dead center. I got him good and it didn't look like he was breathing."

Adams said he was paid off for the hit. LaPlaca told him "Si thinks you did a real fine job, everything is cool."

George's daughter, Mrs. Linda Jane Wright, was present in Inverness on the night of the shooting. She said she was seated at a card table in a basement recreation room with her husband, mother, and father. She said George Jayne was shuffling cards and there was a "boom like a loud explosion from the direction of the window. She recalled that her father stood up slowly, "blood was spurting out all over the place, his eyes were open and then he slumped to the floor." Jayne was rushed to a nearby hospital but he was dead on arrival.

The October 28, 1970, shooting of George Jayne set off a massive police investigation. Agents of the Illinois Bureau of Investigation, known as the IBI, fanned out questioning neighbors about the shooting. It paid off. An 18 year old youth, who was a student at Michigan State University visiting his parents, noticed the car with the hood up. The young man got the first three numbers of the license plates — 9-3-6. It so happened the Adams's Ford had license plates starting with 9-3-6.

Later when he was spotted driving his Ford, having license plates 9-3-6, he was questioned by police about the case. Adams's name had surfaced during the investigation, so he had become one of the targets of the IBI. It so happened that Adams was carrying $10,000 in cash. That piqued the interest of the lawmen. An examination soon revealed that Si Jayne's prints were on 17 of the bills. Adams still played it cool, claiming he knew nothing about the murder.

Enter George Jayne's widow, Marion. She offered a $25,000 reward for information about her husband's killer. Marion, accompanied by IBI agent Dave Hamm, took a satchel with $25,000 in cash and drove to a restaurant where Adams's wife Patricia worked as a waitress. The ploy was effective. Soon Marion and Hamm were showing the reward money to Adams himself. The scheme worked. Adams copped out. He admitted his role in the shooting but insisted Julius Barnes was the triggerman.

Adams never collected the reward money. For a consolation prize he was given immunity from prosecution and would not be charged with any crime, so long as he cooperated with prosecutors.

Adams did tell police the location of the murder weapon. It was hidden in a sewer pipe. Barnes was soon picked up and gave investigators a statement, which was later recanted. Barnes, by the way, had purchased a Cadillac, albeit used, shortly after the shooting and that had raised some eyebrows in his neighborhood as to how a laborer like Barnes could come up with enough money to buy a luxury automobile.

The state now had its ducks in order. In May, 1971, Jayne, LaPlaca, Barnes, and Nefeld were indicted. Nefeld never went to trial. He pleaded guilty to conspiracy to kill the younger Jayne and was sentenced to a three to 10 year jail term.

Si and his confederates were remanded to custody and were kept in prison while awaiting trial, not that Si didn't attempt to make bond. James DeLorto, a veteran agent with the Alcohol, Treasury, and Firearms Department said Jayne always carried a load of gold coins in his money belt if he expected to be arrested. That way Silas could come up with enough "moolah" to post bond. But in this case the judge felt the Jayne crowd was a danger and posed a flight risk. That meant Si would have to call the Cook County Jail home for the next two years.

When the trial finally got underway in the spring of 1973 Jayne had one of the hottest criminal defense attorneys in his corner. That was F. Lee Bailey, who in 1973 was at the height of his powers. When Bailey appeared live one night on a WBBM-TV newscast, anchor Walter Jacobson asked Bailey what he was charging to defend Si. Bailey wouldn't take the bait. Jacobson said he heard it was $250,000, and Walter was right. That was the tab Jayne paid the Bailey team to represent himself, LaPlaca, and Barnes. Bailey's partner Gerald Alch represented LaPlaca, and Chicago attorney George Howard was in Barnes' corner.

For the state the number one chair went to Nick Motherway, a young prosecutor who was planning to go into private practice. The chance to clash swords with Bailey was too big a challenge. Said Motherway, "When they hired F. Lee Bailey, I had to stick around, otherwise it would have looked like I was running away. I couldn't wait to get started." Motherway had a sharp associate, James Schreier, who later became a judge.

The trial finally got underway some two years after the defendants were arrested. It played to a packed house full of court buffs, reporters, lawyers, and the curious eager to see the highly touted Bailey in action.

The state's big gun was Melvin Adams who as we indicated earlier was granted immunity from prosecution in

F. Lee Bailey with John Drummond. Bailey represented Silas Jayne in his 1973 trial. WHO-TV photo.

exchange for his testimony. Prosecutors also had the murder weapon with Barnes's prints on it. And to show motive Motherway had several witnesses who would relate how Si had threatened to murder George.

One witness, a Mrs. Ruth Kinnas, said that in 1961 Silas became enraged after George's horse had won an event. Silas, she said, ran up to George and said "You son of a bitch, I'll kill you." And then as we mentioned earlier, George's daughter testified that Silas had threatened to kill her father.

Bailey gave no opening remarks and when he spoke, he did so with few, if any, notes. He was always brief when he talked, not allowing the jury to let their minds wander.

The state's case rested on the credibility of Adams. If the defense could destroy Adams, Jayne would walk. The defense contended that Adams had concocted his version of events in order to save himself and blame the murders on Jayne, LaPlaca, and Barnes. They argued to the nine women, three men jury that Adams was the actual trigger man. Bailey portrayed Adams as a habitual liar and to bolster the defense view, a police videotape was introduced showing Adams denying to investigators any knowledge of the George Jayne murder. The tape was made during a nine hour interrogation of Adams on November 9, 1970, less than a month after the death of George Jayne and well before Adams began cooperating with authorities. Bailey claimed that Adams calmly lied to police on the tape in the same calm, composed manner that he lied when he testified for the prosecution.

Attorney George Howard who represented Barnes put the father of six on the stand. Barnes alleged that Adams offered him money if he would admit to shooting Jayne. Barnes testified that Adams told him that, he, Adams, killed George Jayne but needed a good alibi and asked Barnes to admit to the murder. According to Barnes, Adams said, "Don't worry about it. I'll get you off." Barnes told the court he was hesitant at first but Adams offered to split $25,000 with him if he went along.

Barnes said he signed a confession at the IBI when Adams walked in and said "tell them all you know, they don't want us, they want Silas Jayne." Barnes as we pointed out later recanted the confession and took his chances with the jury. When asked if he knew anything about guns, the sixth grade dropout replied, "Just loading and shooting."

Bailey had been playing cagey throughout the trial as to whether the trial's main attraction would testify. But the suspense ended on the afternoon of April 24, 1973 when the wealthy horseman took the stand. "Oh, yes," Silas admitted, he had quarreled with his younger brother. However, the defendant claimed the dispute was triggered over the issue of doping horses and not because of competition between the two men in the show ring. Silas testified that he was concerned that George was drugging horses and he feared that the Jayne name could be ruined as a result.

Silas said he once had words with George during a show in Chicago after his brother called him "old-fashioned," but he denied he ever threatened his brother or ever expressed a death wish about him. Silas testified the two men made up and shook hands at a family unity meeting in 1967. Since 1967, the older Jayne said he had no more quarrels with his sibling.

Apparently the jury didn't buy Si's story. Following four weeks of testimony and about eight hours of deliberation, the jury found Jayne and the other defendants guilty.

F. Lee Bailey told reporters outside the courtroom that he had scored a victory. He contended that although the jury had found Jayne guilty of conspiracy to murder it had acquitted him on the more serious charge of murder. Silas was handed down a six to 20 years sentence by Judge Richard Fitzgerald, the maximum under Illinois law for conspiracy. Defendant Joseph LaPlaca, the "go-between" in the murder scheme, also got a six to 20 prison hitch but not before prosecutor Motherway described the handyman as a parasite sucking on the blood money available from Jayne. Triggerman Barnes had to do the most time. He was given a 25 to 35 year prison term.

After the verdict individual jurors were contacted by reporters. One juror, a male, said Si would have gotten first degree murder if his icy stares had not shaken some of the female jurors. According to the male juror, the women panelists would come into the jury room following testimony and in some cases would cry because they were so upset.

The Jayne stare jibes with what Dave Hamm said. Hamm, a longtime state policeman who spent more time investigating Jayne than any other lawman, recalled that Jayne was a guy who could "Scare the pants right off you by just looking at you."

The trial was over and the stories about Jayne and his confederates were no longer front page material but if the public, the media, and law enforcement thought they had heard the last of Silas Jayne, they were mistaken.

Si was transferred from the Cook County Jail to the maximum security Stateville Prison near Joliet. While there Jayne was considered a model prisoner and after only two years in the "Big House" he was sent to the minimum security correctional facility in downstate Vienna, which was then considered the "country club" of the Illinois prison system.

In January of 1978, I received a call from an associate of Jayne asking me if Channel Two would like to interview Silas at his farm near Elgin. It was to be a WBBM-TV exclusive, I was told. It seemed Jayne was being given a furlough to spend a few days with his family. Of course, I jumped at the chance although a new executive producer at the station who was not from Chicago was not very enthusiastic about the Jayne story. A relative newcomer to Chicago, he knew nothing about the Jayne saga and the idea of overtime on a Saturday for me and a camera crew didn't sit too well. However, he reluctantly agreed.

Si was in a gregarious mood at the farm discussing his time in prison and showing us some new stock. It was a great picture story with a wide ranging interview from one of the most controversial figures at the time in the Chicago area. When we returned to the station that Saturday, I assumed we would be putting the piece on the air, pronto. But the executive producer was not impressed saying the interview could wait until the following week.

But other media members were aware that Silas was at his farm. Bob Weidrich, an ace crime reporter, from *The Chicago Tribune* had gotten wind of the furlough. He got in touch with Governor Jim Thompson, no admirer, of Jayne. Thompson said "no dice" to the furlough and ordered Jayne back to prison.

Silas Jayne, during an interview. WBBM-TV photo.

When the *Tribune* bannered the story in its Sunday editions, the regime at Channel Two decided it was a good story after all and we scrambled to put it on the air.

In May, 1979 Jayne was released from prison after spending eight years behind bars, the first two of which were at the Cook County Jail while he was awaiting trial. No sooner was Si out than he in the news again. He was embroiled in a legal dispute after he tried to buy a stable in suburban Northbrook. And then came more woes for Jayne.

He was arrested by federal authorities in May, 1979, seven months after his release from prison. Jayne was accused, while in prison, of plotting to burn the stables of the Homer Adcock farm near Oconomowoc, Wisconsin. The 1976 arson blaze at the Nimrod Stables killed 33 show horses and caused damage estimated at $350,000. Investigators said Silas hired Charles Johnson, a fellow inmate, who worked in the prison kitchen with Jayne, to torch the Nimrod Stables. Law enforcement officials said another Vienna inmate was involved in the plot but died before the case reached the trial stage. As to motive, Justice Department officials said Jayne had told several people that Adcock was "no good" and something had to be done about the owner of the Wisconsin stables.

The Jayne trial was held in downstate Benton, Illinois, because the government contended the alleged plot was hatched in Vienna. The government's case rested upon the testimony of Johnson who told prosecutors that he was paid $5,100 to set fire to the Nimrod stables.

Long before the trial began in the spring of 1980, I received a call from a friend of Jayne who inquired if Channel Two would be interested in doing a videotaped interview with Johnson. Since Johnson was going to be the siege gun in the government's case we quickly accepted the offer. In the 1979 interview Johnson denied being paid by Jayne to set any kind of fire. And for good measure he had nothing but praise for the aging horseman. Apparently Johnson later had second thoughts. He turned out to be the prosecution's star witness after all.

George Howard, Jayne's attorney in the arson case, soon heard about the Johnson interview and he subpoenaed the tape so he could use it at trial. Johnson testified that Jayne had paid him to set the fire in a plot planned when Jayne was doing time at Vienna. Howard then showed the Johnson videotape to the jury of seven men and five women. On the Channel Two tape, Johnson branded as lies that Jayne paid him to torch the Nimrod Farms Stables. Said Johnson in the taped interview, "Si Jayne is my best friend. I think it is part of a gigantic conspiracy to have Silas Jayne die in prison." On the tape I asked Johnson if Jayne ever asked him to set any fires. Johnson replied, "Never."

The jury had to determine which Johnson to believe. The man on the witness stand, or the man who gave the interview. The videotape of the ex-con apparently was the deciding factor. The jury deliberated four hours and 20 minutes before finding Jayne not guilty of conspiring to commit arson and aiding and abetting arson. The TV interview doomed Johnson's credibility. The trial was the last time that Silas Jayne would ever face criminal charges.

Homer Adcock, who considered himself a friend of Jayne, albeit a competitor, was victimized by another fire, three months after the first blaze that had killed 33 horses. The second fire destroyed a number of horses that had been kept in a temporary barn. No charges were ever filed in the second blaze and investigators said at the time that Adcock was reluctant to talk about the second fire.

Although Jayne was never arrested, again his name surfaced in a number of investigations, in some of which he remains a suspect.

Some law enforcement officials are convinced that Silas Jayne masterminded the disappearance of candy heiress Helen Vorhees Brach. Mrs. Brach, the widow of candy mogul Frank Brach, vanished on February 17, 1977, shortly after undergoing a routine physical examination at the Mayo Clinic in Rochester, Minnesota.

Authorities believe Mrs. Brach was murdered and an informant later claimed that her body was disposed of by placing it in the blast furnace of a northwest Indiana steel mill. Jayne was incarcerated at a prison in Vienna when Mrs. Brach disappeared but lawmen believe Jayne was calling the shots from his southern Illinois jail cell.

Mrs. Brach reportedly was going to blow the whistle on some unscrupulous horsemen who had swindled a number of wealthy widows from Chicago's North Shore. Jayne, it was believed, was indirectly involved in some of the transactions that bilked the widow.

On several occasions we asked Silas Jayne if he had anything to do with the wealthy woman's demise. He denied it and also denied knowing anything about it. Jayne was well aware of police suspicions that he had something to do with Mrs. Brach.

So when a former prison mate of Jayne came forward and told police that after he was paroled in 1977, he buried the "candy lady" near the Twin Cities of Minneapolis and Saint Paul. The name "candy lady" was a term used by some people when they referred to Mrs. Brach. The prisoner, Maurice Ferguson, was doing time in a Mississippi prison when he came forward and told authorities that he had been paid to take the Brach body from Illinois and rebury the remains in Minnesota. Ferguson's story had some plausibility since Mrs. Brach had disappeared in Minnesota. So Ferguson was brought to the Twin Cities on what turned out to be a wild goose chase. Not only lawmen but also the media, including this writer, went along for the ride.

The Ferguson affair turned out to be a complete hoax. Ferguson was flown from the prison in Parchman, Mississippi, on a three day pass. After combing through five area cemeteries and checking out other tips from Ferguson, no body was ever found. Officials said Ferguson had lied just to get out of prison for a few days. As one put it, "This is like a trip to Club Med for him."

It was hardly a Club Med experience for the lawmen and media members who had to traipse through snow covered fields in a Minnesota winter. January in the Twin Cities is not exactly like Palm Beach. Authorities believe Ferguson never brought Brach's body to the Twin Cities area. Ferguson's last words before boarding an Illinois State Police plane that would take him back to Mississippi were, "I enjoyed Minnesota." Several Illinois lawmen I talked to are convinced that Silas had put Ferguson up to the scheme and that Jayne had the last laugh after all.

Silas Jayne's name also surfaced in one of the most sensational homicides in Chicago history, the Schuessler-Peterson case. Thirteen year John Schuessler, his eleven year old brother, Anton, and their friend, fourteen year old Robert Peterson, had gone bowling at a northwest side lanes on October 16, 1955. Two days later a grim discovery was made. The naked bodies of the three boys, all strangled were found in a forest preserve.

Some 40 years after the murders a south suburban horseman, Kenneth Hansen was convicted of the slayings. Investigators believe the murders took place at a northwest side stables then owned by Silas Jayne. A prosecution witness at the 1995 trial said he was told that Silas helped dispose of the bodies in the forest preserve. There is some dispute as to whether Hansen was an employee of Jayne. Silas' widow, Dorothy, testified at Hansen's second trial that the defendant had never worked at the Idle Hour Stables, the "Jayne-owned" property, which was the alleged site of the slayings. Former state policeman Dave Hamm testified that Hansen told him that he went to work at the Jayne stables in 1955, the year of the murders.

However, there can be no question that Hansen was at least an associate of Jayne. In fact, Hansen was arrested and then released in connection with the 1970 shooting of George Jayne. Silas was never charged in the Schuessler–Peterson case although suspicion remains even until this day that Jayne was involved after the boys were slain.

Silas Jayne's name, rightly or wrongly, always seemed to crop up in several criminal matters. There was the July, 1966, disappearance of three young women who vanished after spending the day at the Indiana Dunes State Park in northwest Indiana. Twenty-one year old Ann Miller of Lombard, 19 year old Renee Bruhl of Chicago, and 19 year old Patricia Blough of Westchester were last seen getting into a blue and white speed boat. At least that's what one witness thought he saw.

The three young women were all enthusiastic horsewomen who had frequented George Jayne's Tri-Color Stables, the site of a 1965 bombing that killed Cheryl Rude. Investigators theorized the three young women may have seen someone planting a bomb in George Jayne's car. That was the bomb that killed Rude. In other words they knew too much.

In examining purses and other personal effects of the three young women, police found several items of interest: George Jayne's phone number and the number of Si's first wife. But trying to tie Silas Jayne to the Dunes' disappearance may be a little far fetched. The young women could have drowned, could have been in a boating accident, could have staged their own disappearance, or met with foul play not connected to anything that concerned Silas Jayne. At any rate the disappearance of the three young women in 1966 apparently is no closer to being solved than it was some forty years ago.

Silas, however, had civil problems. George Jayne's widow, Marion won a million dollar judgment against him after Silas was convicted of murdering her husband. Si said he was nearly broke and was not in a position to pay the fee, but Jayne did raise money after he got out of jail to buy a stable. Silas reportedly told friends that he owned some 4,000 acres of land in Australia. But several attempts to purchase a stable ran into legal problems.

Jayne, though, in his last years continued his love affair with horses. He was involved in polo matches at the old Chicago Armory. I recall him urging Channel Two to cover the matches which were held on Saturdays. He felt polo was a great game and it did not get the media coverage it deserved.

Silas Jayne lived quietly until his death from leukemia on July 13, 1987. He was 80 years old. There was no fanfare when Jayne died. In fact, family members at first denied he had passed away. Perhaps relatives did want the media to dredge old stories about the Cain and Abel relationship between Silas and George.

One of Silas's co-defendants did not go quietly. Julius Barnes who was the triggerman in the George Jayne murder was himself a shooting victim in 1992. The 58 year old Barnes got into an altercation with another man and was shot to death with a .38 caliber handgun. The killer and Barnes were quarreling over a dog when the argument got out hand.

Silas Jayne used the media when he could. There was no question that Channel Two and I were partially responsible for Jayne's acquittal in the Wisconsin arson case. Without the tape interview of the alleged arsonist who claimed Jayne had nothing to do with the fire, Silas probably would have spent the rest of his life in prison. The Charles Johnson interview was newsworthy and I contend any other news organization, print or electronic, would have done the same thing.

Silas Jayne, or Si as most every one called him, was an enigma. He could play the favorite uncle role and put on the charm when he wanted to or he could be ruthless and vicious. Those who were perceived by Jayne as rivals saw only the dark side. The few that considered themselves friends of Si, saw an affable horse breeder who was being bum rapped by the media.

Those in law enforcement saw Silas Jayne as a mentor of murder and mayhem, a person who believed violence could solve any dispute.

3

THE CONSPIRACY THEORIST

Sherman Skolnick lost credibility after a United Airlines crash. WBBM-TV photo.

If there was ever a guy who should be in the "grassy knoll club" it would be Sherman Skolnick. Sherman was a real conspiracy theorist. A modern day chicken little, who was always saying the sky was falling.

To his friends he was a crusader against corruption, always controversial, perhaps a political gadfly but to others less charitable, he was a crackpot—scurrilous, irresponsible, and a faker. His Committee To Clean Up The Courts was at times only a one man operation. But there was a period that the media in Chicago fawned over Skolnick. That was in the late 1960s and early 1970s.

His charges in 1969 led to the resignations of Illinois Supreme Court Justices Roy Solfisburg and Ray Klingbiel in one of the biggest judicial scandals in Illinois history. Skolnick had contended that the two jurists had accepted a gift of stock in a Chicago bank. The problem, Skolnick said, was that the gift came from a defendant whose case was being heard by the two justices. It was a clear case of conflict of interest and it didn't help the judges' cause when they ruled in favor of the defendant. The judicial scandal made Skolnick and he became a local celebrity overnight. But Sherm was just getting started.

It was about that time (1969) that Skolnick filed a law suit which eventually led to the re-districting of Illinois congressional districts. Sherm also contended that information he provided to the government eventually led to the corruption trial and conviction of Federal Appeals Court Judge Otto Kerner, the former Illinois governor. How much of a role Skolnick played in the Kerner affair is a matter of debate. Some Justice Department figures insist that Skolnick had little or no influence in the Kerner case.

At any rate, it was then that Skolnick could snap his fingers and reporters would scramble to his house in the 98 hundred block of South Oglesby, hoping to get a scoop or at least a tidbit.

Sherman Skolnick was born in Chicago in 1930, right at the start of the depression. His parents were Jewish immigrants who settled on the west side with their three sons. The family was not wealthy and Sherman's father toiled as a tailor, while his mother was a homemaker. When Sherm was six years old, tragedy struck. Young Skolnick contracted polio while the family was vacationing in Benton Harbor, Michigan.

Polio was often deadly and debilitating in that era and despite a number of operations Sherman spent the bulk of his life in a wheelchair. Although he was wheelchair bound Skolnick did not let his handicap interfere with his schooling. He went to Loop College, DePaul University, and finally John Marshall Law School, but didn't finish.

That's when he started describing himself as a legal researcher and a corruption crusader. His physical limitations may have been a motive in Skolnick's desire to excel. He moved to the south side where he maintained what he called "the hottest phones in town," giving residents what he described as news the monopoly press would not or could not cover. Skolnick had reporters paying him homage until 1973. That's when he went off the deep end and lost much of his credibility.

In December of 1972, a United Airlines Jet crashed near Midway Airport killing all 45 persons on board. One of the passengers was Mrs. Howard Hunt, wife of one of the Watergate burglars. Skolnick said the plane had been sabotaged and said he had the evidence to support that claim.

The National Transportation Board held hearings on the crash, with Skolnick one of the star witnesses. Skolnick was in his glory in those days and he relished it. Here he had a chance to shine in the national spotlight. Skolnick never looked like a matinee idol but he took steps to make him appear more presentable when he showed up under the lights at the NTSB hearing. Some reporters had cruelly dubbed Skolnick as Quasimodo because of his cow catcher teeth. But he had those teeth fixed and was brimming with confidence when his big day finally arrived.

Sherman really swung for the fences. He told investigators that the FBI, CBS, traffic controllers at Midway, and United Airlines had hushed up what had happened. He charged that President Nixon had placed a hit man on the plane to make certain that Mrs. Hunt died. But Skolnick could offer no proof or any documentation to support his sensational charges. As one observer put it, "His statement had no factual basis, and he couldn't support his position other than with rhetoric." I covered the hearing and recall the chuckles and snickers from the audience as Skolnick detailed his allegations of conspiracy.

From then on it was all downhill for Sherman. Of course it didn't help the Skolnick cause when he vanished before the

NTSB hearing. One of Skolnick's aides reported to police that Sherm and his driver had disappeared. According to a Skolnick associate, Sherm and his driver had left Skolnick's house in a red station wagon at 8:15 A.M. on a Monday morning. Sherman had left orders to report him missing if he did not return or call an associate by 9:15 A.M. The associate went so far as to say that Skolnick had been kidnapped and was being held prisoner by cutthroats trying to obtain secret information that only Skolnick possessed.

Reporters wondered if Skolnick had met with foul play. After all he alleged that he had many enemies who would like to do him in. Sherman had said that "powerful forces" had wanted him to turn over his files in the Watergate matter.

The truth of Skolnick's disappearance came out three days after he had vanished. Skolnick and his associate turned up in a Windsor, Ontario, motel where they had gone to seek political asylum. Skolnick explained to Canadian authorities that he had left Chicago because he feared he was going to be arrested or tossed into a mental hospital. The southsider said he had incriminating information regarding Attorney General John Mitchell's role in the 1972 Watergate "break-in." Mitchell did indeed do time in connection with Watergate, but Skolnick alleged that he had been threatened by FBI agents if he didn't turn over the Watergate documents.

The scenario then switched to the Dirksen Federal Building in Chicago when the U.S. Attorney for the Northern District of Illinois, Jim Thompson, promised Skolnick amnesty if he would return to Chicago. Skolnick at first smelled treachery saying that amnesty could be a trick. However, Thompson assured Skolnick that if he came back no criminal charges would be filed against him and he would not be put into a mental hospital.

The fear that Skolnick had been kidnapped proved groundless, and was a body blow to the Skolnick mystique. The media's love affair with Sherman was over. True, Skolnick continued to operate the "hottest phones in town" and continued to file charges of public corruption on the Chicago scene but the media wasn't taking Sherman seriously any more.

But Skolnick would surface when major stories about corruption broke. When the federal Greylord indictment came down linking Chicago judges to corruption, Skolnick was at the Dan Webb news conference where the charges were announced. Sherman did a little chest thumping then, contending that he knew such activity had been going for years. So did a number of other people who had been urging the federal authorities to clamp down on corrupt Cook County Judges. Skolnick played little or no role in the Greylord case.

We did a lengthy profile at Channel Two on Skolnick in 1979 shortly after the crash of American Airlines Flight 191. The DC-10 had gone down shortly after taking off from O'Hare Field on a flight to Los Angeles. All aboard the huge plane were killed in one of the worst aviation disasters in U.S. history.

Sherman was in high gear arguing that Flight 191 had been sabotaged, just like the United Airlines plane that went down near Midway seven years before. Again, like his appearance before the NTSB in 1973, he could offer no proof to back up his claim.

We chatted with Skolnick in front of his south side home. He did not allow us to go into his house that served as his command post and was well camouflaged from the street by underbrush and weeds. Sherm told us that donations and lecture fees kept him and his organization, The Citizens Committee To Clean Up The Courts, in business. He was also getting a monthly check from Social Security.

His telephone messages were of shotgun style, hoping some of the pellets would hit home, but most of his allegations were wide of the mark.

A year after our TV profile, Skolnick charged this writer with setting up the assassination of mob hitman Billy Dauber and his wife Charlotte. Well, we were at the Will County Court-house in Joliet when the Daubers departed the building after a brief court appearance. However we were at the courthouse with a Channel Two News crew to get fresh video of Dauber, not to finger him for death. Had we known that Dauber was going to be slain after the hearing we would have followed the Dauber car down a rural road where he met his demise.

Several others I've known were so outraged by Skolnick's libelous attacks on them that they threatened to sue. But they cooled off after attorneys told them that Skolnick probably didn't have any money, that only a few listened to his phone messages, and that if they sued, the mainstream media would report it, giving some credibility to Skolnick's charges. Suing the barristers argued, would be counterproductive.

Don't get the idea that Sherm was never sued. In 1975 Skolnick was sued by two attorneys whom Sherman said had bribed a divorce judge. A year later, Circuit Court Judge Paul Elward found Skolnick guilty of libel following some verbal fireworks by the legal researcher. During one heated exchange Skolnick compared the judge to Hitler saying, "I feel the same way addressing you as Jews did 30 years ago addressing Adolph Hitler." Whether the two lawyers ever got any money from Sherman is unknown, but it must have been like squeezing blood out of a turnip.

Despite those reverses Skolnick was still firing from the hip. When Jimmy Hoffa vanished in July, 1975 Skolnick said he had information that Hoffa was buried in Michigan's Upper Peninsula. The Teamster leader's body was never found in the U.P.

Everybody was fair game for Skolnick. Sherman charged that WBBM-TV shook down Dominck's, a big supermarket chain in the Chicago area, in order to get more commercials from the firm. Skolnick argued that of Mayor (to be) Jane Byrne's transition team, were mostly military intelligence and CIA. Here was another outlandish message: the mysterious

Raoul of James Earl Ray fame ran a truck hi-jacking operation for what Skolnick called corrupt FBI agents. Other recorded phone commentaries were also off the wall. Skolnick was becoming known as a crackpot.

Then in 1987 Skolnick tried to hit the jackpot. In November, Mayor Harold Washington died of a massive heart attack. That's what Cook County Medical Examiner Robert Stein announced after an autopsy on the Mayor's body.

Skolnick, though, had other ideas. His information, which he said came from unnamed informants, hinted that Washington was murdered. Skolnick claimed that a toxicology report showed there was cocaine in the Mayor's bloodstream. Skolnick's view caused something of an uproar. Dr. Stein called Skolnick's reports irresponsible. So too did close friends and relatives of Washington. After his Washington charges Skolnick pretty much disappeared from public view for a time.

True, he continued to record several messages each week on his hot line but he had lost so much credibility that he was pretty much ignored by both the press and public. Skolnick also became more concerned about his physical condition, never wanting to be photographed in his wheel chair. That hampered him from making appearances in public.

Skolnick though tried something of a comeback in recent years. He had his own internet site so he was able to speak out against what he perceived as corruption and wrongdoing. I was going to do another Skolnick piece in 2001 but the powers that be at Channel Two decided that Skolnick was "old hat" and no longer newsworthy. I remember Sherman giving me one last "goodie" at that time. He claimed that missing Congressional intern Chaundra Levy, "seemed to be a penetration agent for Israeli intelligence."

Skolnick was plagued by health problems in that era. He fell down the stairs at his home and his last days were spent with a live-in caregiver. In May, 2006, when Sherman was 75 years old, he died of an apparent heart attack.

While Skolnick was dismissed in his later years as a crack-pot, it didn't start out that way. Skolnick may have been thought of as a modern day Don Quixote tilting windmills but you have to give "the devil his due." It was Skolnick and not some special commission who first charged two justices of the Illinois Supreme Court with improper conduct. And Skolnick was persistent in his allegations of judicial misconduct well before the Greylord investigation got underway.

But Sherman later went off the tracks with his shotgun style of attack on perceived wrongdoing. He became the butt of jokes and laughed at because of his paranoia. In many ways it was sad, because I remember those halcyon days in 1969 if Skolnick spoke, you listened.

4

THE CRIMINAL LAWYER

Julius Lucius Echeles, a very colorful barrister.
WBBM-TV photo.

In a city that has had its share of colorful criminal lawyers, Julius Lucius Echeles certainly was one of the most
flamboyant. He represented everyone from John Doe types to
syndicate figures such as "Jimmy the Monk" Allegretti, Sam
DeStefano, Richard Cain, and Ronald DeAngeles. Because
he represented more than his share of Outfit clients he was
called in some circles, "The Mob's Mouthpiece," a nom de
guerre that Echeles resented.

Once when he appeared on a Channel Two Sunday interview show, called "Newsmakers," Echeles was asked at the outset of the taping, by the host Walter Jacobson, if he was the "mob's mouthpiece."Echeles replied indignantly, "Mr. Jacobson, that is pure, unadulterated bullshit."

The show's producer Winifred Chambers dashed out of the control room and informed Julius. "You can't say that on the air." Echeles turned around and innocently said, "You told me I could say anything."

Jacobson always started the show by asking the guest either a tough question or something that would rile him or her up. The idea was not to lob a soft question at the guest but something that might provide a newsworthy answer. In other words start the show off with a bang to grab the viewer's attention.

After Echeles' frank reply, the taping began again, only this time Walter's question was a bit milder. The show though was a success. Of course you couldn't go wrong when you had a guest like Julius he was a show in itself.

Julius Lucius Echeles was born in 1915 on Chicago's west side. He grew up in modest circumstances. His father, the family's breadwinner, was a blacksmith, a trade you don't hear much about these days. By the time Julius attended high school (he went to Tuley) he was an avid reader, with Charles Dickens listed as his favorite author. Long after his school days were over he delighted in quoting from Dickens. Echeles went to junior college for two years before enrolling at Chicago Law School. By then the Depression was taking its toll. Bad times caused the law school to fold. But Echeles was persistent in his bid to become a barrister. He went to night school at John Marshall Law School and passed the bar exam without a college diploma or law degree. Echeles was on his way.

Julius's career as a young attorney hit a temporary roadblock when World War II began. Actually the service stint may have helped his career in the long run. He joined the

Navy and found his niche as a criminal lawyer when he successfully defended a young sailor on rape charges. With the sailor's acquittal in the back of his mind, Echeles knew what kind of lawyer he wanted to be when he was mustered out of the service.

Back in civilian life he soon attracted attention by defending a number of individuals facing various marijuana charges. Before long, Echeles had quite a reputation when it came to drug cases. He was getting acquittals and that helped business, and his style didn't go unnoticed either. Who else but Echeles would belt out an operatic aria during an appearance before the state Supreme Court. And it was Echeles who once stunned a courtroom by getting down on his knees to present his closing arguments.

Julius's rapid fire rhetoric more often than not would convince a jury of his client's innocence. But Echeles lost his share of cases, too, and as he told me in a 1979 interview: "I don't know if there are tricks to the game. There are of course procedural activities that we engage in. It's a presentation. It's rapport with the jury. It's presenting your client's case in the best possible light, after having put the witnesses on the stand or having cross examined the witnesses for the prosecution. The criminal cases are subtle. That is, jurors decide cases on factors we don't always know about."

Echeles's career as an attorney almost came to an end in 1954 when he went off the straight and narrow and was convicted of conspiracy to bribe the Chicago Postmaster for job promotions. Judge Julius Hoffman, of Chicago 7 fame, sentenced Echeles to 28 months in a federal penitentiary. The term was later reduced to 22 months. Echeles did his time at the federal pen in Terre Haute, Indiana, and ended up serving only nine months. When Julius got out, a number of attorneys, prosecutors, and judges went to bat for Echeles and he was reinstated to the practice of law.

Julius hung out his shingle again with many of his clients involved in drug violations. His practice was pretty much the same as it was before he went to jail. But that all changed after Echeles represented a police officer who had been indicted in the famed Summerdale scandal, in which police officers were serving as lookouts for a burglar. The trial garnered heavy newspaper coverage and Julius's colorful style and his sharp exchanges with prosecutors netted him a degree of notoriety.

The Outfit brass apparently took note and before long his retinue of clients included a bevy of crime syndicate figures. They included, as we mentioned earlier, Rush Street boss Allegretti, ex-cop Cain, enforcer DeStefano, and wire tap expert DeAngeles. It was then that some fellow attorneys, perhaps a bit jealous of Julius's success, described him as the mob's mouthpiece. Granted, Echeles had his share of mob clients, but there were other Chicago attorneys who had more. It would be incorrect to describe Julius as the "mob's mouthpiece." Most of his criminal practice involved ordinary Joes who you would see traipsing through the halls of the Criminal Courts Building on their way to a date with a judge.

During a lengthy interview we once asked Echeles about the "mob mouthpiece" allegations and he replied. "I've never been accused of being anybody's man. The accusations against me are that I'm too independent. I represent persons who come to me. If they have the sobriquet that the newspapers or news media put on them, that's no deterrent to my representing them, if they are able to pay me. Luckily most have been able to pay me, although some such as Sam DeStefano and Richard Cain went to their demise too early before they were able to pay their just legal fees."

When Echeles lamented the demise of clients DeStefano and Cain he was referring to the spectacular murders of both men. DeStefano was slain on April 14, 1973, while in his garage. He was found sprawled on the cement floor with multiple shotgun wounds in the chest and left arm. DeStefano was awaiting trial for murder when he was gunned down. Investigators theorized that Sam had been lured into believing he was going on a hit to silence a witness who was scheduled to testify against him. There was a hit all right, but Sam was the target and not the witness.

Eight months later Cain, a former Sheriff's Policeman, met a grisly fate in a west side sandwich shop. Cain was murdered on December 20, 1973, by two masked gunmen who shot him twice in the face with shotguns. The slaying occurred around noontime as horrified witnesses looked on. The murders of the two men were never solved.

DeStefano, known as the "Mad Hatter of the underworld," was a mercurial client who would blow up over nothing. He once sent one of his henchmen to kill Julius, after the two men had quarreled. The henchman never carried out his murderous assignment and later went into the witness protection program. Although Echeles was never harmed physically by DeStefano, he was the recipient of several tongue lashings by Sam.

Echeles had a great sense of street smarts. He knew what was going on. I recall seeing him over at the Criminal Courts Building one day. By then he was sporting a beard and he came up to me and said, "Listen Drummond, something big is going on over here, the Feds are asking a lot of questions about some of the judges. I think you ought to know about it." Julius was referring to the Greylord investigation, in which a number of judges, lawyers, and courtroom personnel were indicted on corruption charges. Echeles had gotten wind of the probe long before it became public.

In later years Echeles became less active as he was plagued by a number of physical problems. He walked with a cane because of a toe infection and some circulatory issues. He had heart disease and suffered from emphysema. But he was as quick with a quip as ever. His office was now in his apartment at Marina City.

Yet he would often show up at the Dirksen Federal Building when an interesting trial was in progress. And when Julius arrived in the courtroom there was a buzz in the audience. Court buffs would surround him during recess, asking for words of wisdom about how the case was going. Prosecutors and defense attorneys would also stop by, hoping he would give kudos to their courtroom work.

In the mid-90s Echeles had given up his practice and moved to Pompano Beach, Florida. But Julius didn't get much of a chance to enjoy his golden years. In September, 1998, Echeles died in a Florida hospital following a bout of heart failure and diabetes.

He once told Bill Brashler, of *The Chicago Tribune*, that if he died, "I want it to be on a crap table in Las Vegas while making love to a beautiful woman." Julius didn't get that last wish but he packed more than his share of excitement into his 83 years.

5

THE THOUGHT
PHOTOGRAPHER

Ted Serios is one of life's floaters, a drifter, who washes away the years with shots and beer chasers. Job wise he never struck it big. He worked for a time at the Conrad Hilton Hotel in Chicago, toiling there as a bellhop and elevator starter.

But Ted got his 15 minutes of fame because, according to him, he could look into a camera and take a picture, not of himself, but of the image in his mind. Yes, Ted claimed he was one of the few people on earth who possessed this psychic power. He said he was a thought photographer. Basically Serios boasted that he could look into the lens of a Polaroid

Ted Serios

camera, concentrate on a subject, and presto, 60 seconds later an image would appear on his print.

When we were doing our Chicago Chronicles series on WBBM-TV back in 1979, one Serios pal contacted us and said that we had to see this guy in action.

The viewer went on to describe the Serios act with a camera as "incredible." That was too tempting to resist. We opted to give the Serios story a shot.

So, producer Dave Finney, camera in hand, was dispatched to see if Serios had this uncanny power of causing chemical changes in the emulsion of the photographic plate. A minicam crew accompanied Finney to record the momentous event for posterity.

Finney was shown a number of pictures Serios had allegedly produced over the years. Pictures, Serios said, were produced by transferring images from his brain to film. Ted said he didn't know who the people were who appeared on the pictures. However, Ted had made those pictures without any witnesses.

Finney, though, wanted to see what Serios could do that day. He asked for a demonstration of thought photography. Serios obliged, putting his hand over his forehead, he began grunting and looked closely into the lens of the Polaroid camera. Alas, nothing happened. The photo session was a failure. Was Serios a phony involved in chicanery? Well, Serios had his supporters.

One of these was Dr. Jule Eisenbud, a psychiatrist and psychic researcher, who was associated with the University of Colorado's Medical School. Eisenbud witnessed a demonstration by Serios at a Loop hotel and concluded that Serios was no phony. Several years later Eisenbud, apparently convinced that Serios was the "real McCoy," wrote a book entitled, "The World Of Ted Serios." In the book the author said, in effect, that Serios could indeed photograph mental images

But then a national magazine came out with a story that was not charitable to Serios. *Popular Photography* debunked the whole idea and called Eisenbud naïve. The magazine said it wasn't sure whether Serios was a charlatan or psychic but said it was skeptical. The article killed a grant that would have paid for more experiments with Serios.

Ted claimed he never tried to pull the wool over anybody's eyes. He said he started photographing his mental images around 1954 when he was hypnotized as a joke. A few days later he told the hypnotist that he had begun to see things. The hypnotist laughed at that and told Ted to go home and photograph his visions. Serios came back, he says, with photos of buried treasure. Nobody ever found the buried treasure but Serios continued his passion with thought photography, taking pictures and attracting a few followers. Those who were in the serious camp were true believers. You could not convince them that Ted was a fake. Serios showed us a number of pictures but they were made outside our presence, so we were never able to see Serios actually score.

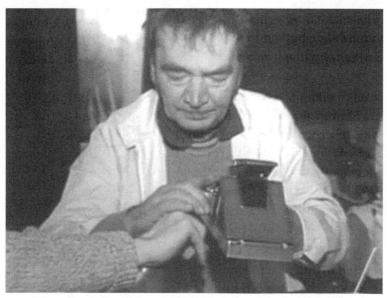

Serios: The real McCoy, or a con man? WBBM-TV photo.

The Serios story appeared on our air in late May, 1979. Audience reaction was strong. Viewers wanted to see more Serios. Some of them wanted more laughs, some were curious or fascinated by what Serios claimed he could do, while still others may have felt that Serious knew what he was talking about.

Ted was no shrinking violet and was not adverse to any more publicity. So, it was no surprise when Serios called the station, contending he had recently had a vision, which he said revealed the body of a missing girl buried in a forest preserve. Ted alleged that the vision came suddenly, "like a bolt out of the blue." Serios tried to copy the vision on a piece of paper, drawing a crude map of the scene.

We were reluctant at first to do another Serious story so soon after airing the first one. Then again if Ted could solve the mystery of the suburban girl who had vanished after attending a rock concert in 1976, it would help the authorities and bring closure to the family. The missing girl was Barbara Glueckert, a teenager from the northwest suburbs (we deal with her story in another section of this book). Not that I expected Serios to succeed. It was a long shot but we felt obligated to give it a try.

We accompanied Serios to an area along the Des Plaines River near the suburb of Wheeling. Ted surmised the body was buried in some bushes in a forest preserve adjacent to the river. He couldn't pinpoint the exact site and after hoofing around several acres no trace of any body was found.

But Serios was not to be denied. He suggested visiting his favorite watering hole on North Clark Street. There he was hopeful with the aid of a couple of "cold ones," thought photography could produce an image of the alleged burial scene. So we adjourned to his favorite haunt and after a few beers Ted gave it his all. Grunting and groaning Serios struck out. Six tries of thought photography failed to produce anything resembling a photo.

Serios, though, wasn't discouraged and ordered another beer insisting he could locate the burial scene. We didn't stick around and left before Ted could begin some serious drinking at our expense. I last remember Ted sitting at the bar quaffing down another beer that made Milwaukee famous. Serios, by the way, never was able to produce on film any resemblance to a burial site.

As to Serios, we soon lost track of him and for that matter we never heard anymore about thought photography. Serios, himself, dropped off the face of the map. He reportedly left Chicago and moved to somewhere in Florida. If Ted is alive today he would be about 87 years old.

6

THE MAN OF STEEL

They called him "The Man of Steel," the hardest hitting middleweight since Stanley Ketchel. A vicious body puncher and knockout artist, Tony Zale was a class act in a business filled with unsavory characters. Zale was middleweight champion of the world in the 1940s, an era that some boxing devotees call "The Golden Age."

Yet, despite his ring skills and a nice guy persona, Zale was never able to cash in on his ring fame like his contemporaries Rocky Graziano and Jake LaMotta.

Born Anthony Florian Zaleski, Tony came out of the Gary steel mills to win the 160 pound class title in 1940. Zale was born to Polish immigrant parents on May 29, 1913, and grew up within sight of Gary's famous steel mills. Those mills soon became a major part of Tony's life because at an early age he had to become one of the family's breadwinners.

The future champ's father, Joseph, was killed when Zale was only two years old. The elder Zaleski was fatally injured when he was struck by a car while riding his bike home from a drug store where he had picked up some medicine for his little son, who was ill. The death of Tony's father left his wife Katherine, with at least four children to raise. It's unclear how many children there were in the Zaleski brood, but there were at least four boys.

Tony Zale, a hard-hitting 160 pounder.

Like other Gary youngsters who grew up in the 1920s or 1930s Tony got a job in the steel mills. It was tough work and Tony hated it. He told me he had to get up at the crack of dawn and spend his shift near blast furnaces catching hot rivets.

Boxing was big in the depression era and soon the Zale boys were pushing leather in the simon pure ranks, but it was Tony, who had the potential and desire to succeed in the rugged game that was professional boxing. As a teenager Tony started working out at Johnny Coulon's gym on Chicago's south side. The diminutive Coulon, a former bantamweight champion and veteran of ninety seven pro bouts was ring wise and able to help Tony in the finer points of the game.

Initially his mother didn't know of Tony's activities in the squared circle, so he changed his name to Zale so she wouldn't recognize it. Zale had ninety five fights as an amateur, winning eighty seven, fifty by knockout. He won the Golden Gloves lightweight championship of Indiana and in 1932 was runner up in the Chicago Golden Gloves tournament.

In 1934, Zale turned pro and had twenty one bouts that year, as many as some fighters today have in a career. He was overmatched several times, facing boxers with much more experience. He grew discouraged, quit the fight game and went back to the steel mills.

For two years Zale toiled near the blast furnaces building up strength on his five foot eight inch frame. His sculpted body was rock hard. It was inevitable that he would give boxing one more shot and there wasn't an ounce of fat on Zale when he climbed back into the ring in 1937. In three years he would become a champion. In his comeback Zale had two sharp managers, Sam Pian and Art Winch. They brought the Gary native along slowly, building up his confidence fighting four and six rounders against lesser lights.

Zale though still had plenty to learn. Jimmy Clark caught him cold and knocked him out in the first round of a 1938 bout in Chicago. But then Zale developed a right cross to go with his vicious left hook. In two rematches he kayoed Clark both times. Zale was on his way.

In 1940 he scored a ten round decision over the one hundred and sixty pound champion Al Hostak in a non title bout in Chicago. Six months later Zale proved his win over Hostak was no fluke. He stopped Al in the thirteenth round of a title go in Seattle, Washington, Hostak's home town.

Zale, long after he had hung up the gloves, always maintained that Hostak was the hardest hitter he had ever faced.

So at the age of twenty-seven Zale was the middleweight champion of the world, that is everywhere but in New York state.

Nine days before Pearl Harbor, Zale won a fifteen round decision over George Abrams at Madison Square Garden to gain universal recognition. Then in his last match for four years he lost a twelve round decision to a much bigger opponent, light-heavyweight champion Billy Conn.

Tony was at his peak when World War II broke out. But like many other boxers of that era Zale traded in his ring trunks for G.I. issue. The champion spent almost four years in the Navy and when he returned to civilian life, he was almost thirty three years old. Zale, said the experts, was over the hill.

While Tony toiled as a gob during the war a young middleweight had caught the fancy of New York's fight faithful. He was Rocky Graziano, a dead-end kid from New York's lower east side, who had scored a number of knockouts against over matched welterweights. Graziano was a brawler, whose cave man ring tactics and string of kayoes was the talk of fistiana.

While Zale presented a clean cut All American boy image, Graziano personified what was wrong with some of America's youth. He had a criminal record, had gone AWOL from the Army for a year, had gotten a dishonorable discharge, and made a practice of hanging out with hoodlums. Although there were better middleweights than Graziano, Rocky was a tremendous drawing card, and a Zale–Graziano bout was a promoters' dream.

The wise guys along "Jacobs Beach," a stretch of concrete near the famous Stillman's gym didn't give Zale much of a chance. They said the kid was too much for the fighter from Gary. Graziano was a two to one favorite.

Close to forty thousand fans were on hand at Yankee stadium on a late September evening in 1946 to see the widely heralded match. And the throng was not disappointed. The two one hundred and sixty pounders went after each other with hammer and tongs. Zale was decked in the second round.

He was bleeding from the mouth and his legs were rubbery. Rocky looked like a sure winner.

Legendary columnist Damon Runyon, sitting at ringside, but suffering from terminal throat cancer, passed a note to a fellow scribe saying "Zale is through." Runyon, however, failed to consider Zale's fighting heart and spirit.

Despite the battering Zale rallied in the sixth round. A right to the heart and a left to the chin put Rocky on the canvas. Although the challenger almost beat the count, the fight was over. Zale though looked more like the loser. He had to be assisted from the ring. Zale was near collapse.

Tony's effort in retaining his crown paid off. He was named fighter of the year by *Ring* magazine, then the Bible of boxing. *Ring* also declared the sixth round of the Zale-Graziano match as the round of the year.

There had to be a rematch and a year later, on a hot summer night at the Chicago Stadium, Graziano turned the tables on Zale. The stadium resembled a Turkish bath on that hot July night. But despite the heat more than eighteen thousand fans paid their way into the old west side arena. The fight grossed four hundred and twenty two thousand dollars, which at the time was the biggest gate ever for a middleweight title bout.

The fight was another "pier six" brawl. Rocky was down in the third round from a hard right but the New Yorker soon turned the tide. And Zale began to wilt. In the sixth round seven rights took the starch out of Tony. He sagged over the middle rope and referee Behr stopped the fight giving Graziano a six round TKO. In several interviews with this writer Zale always insisted that it was the heat and not Graziano's punches that caused him to run out of gas.

The win catapulted the twenty six year old Graziano into the national spotlight. He became a media favorite, was cast as Martha Raye's boyfriend on her popular TV show, and he co-authored a book, *Somebody Up There Likes Me,* which later became a movie starring Paul Newman. Graziano also appeared in a number of movies including several with Frank Sinatra.

Here was Tony Zale an All American boy type who fought for his country getting the brush off from the media and the Broadway crowd while Graziano, an ex-con, who got a dishonorable discharge from the army, was being treated royally. It bothered Tony and really stuck in the craw of Tony's wife. Perhaps that's one reason why the ex-champion worked over Rocky in their rubber match a year later in 1948.

Unlike the heat of the Chicago Stadium there were cool breezes from the Jersey meadows when Zale climbed through the ropes at Ruppert Stadium in Newark. The third Zale-Graziano fight has been seen by more people than any other bout with the exception of several heavyweight contests. That's because it has been given saturation coverage on television through the years.

Like the previous two matches, the pace was torrid from the beginning. Rocky was down in the first round only to get up and face a barrage of punches. Then in the second round Rocky's bombs caused the challenger's knees to buckle.

However, the third round proved to be a disaster for the titleholder. Zale in a sensational manner began battering Rocky at will. As Graziano explained, "a left hook flies at my jaw, then a right cross and I can't move. I'm paralyzed." Rocky said it felt as if his head had fallen six stories onto cement.

It was a convincing victory for Zale, who always contended he was the better man than Rocky. By now Tony had the aura of invincibility. But it was short lived.

Zale was matched with Marcel Cerdan in an outdoor fight in September of 1948. The champion was a heavy favorite to stop the Frenchman, but it was not to be.

From the beginning it was obvious that age had caught up with the thirty-five year old champion. Tony had gone to the well one time too many. Zale's punches lacked steam and only

Tony Zale, former Middleweight Champion during the 1940s and John Drummond. WHO-TV photo.

in the fourth round did Zale look like he could put Cerdan away. Marcel's body punches weakened the Gary native. By the end of the eleventh round Zale could no longer lift his arms. The Hoosier was completely exhausted and dropped to the canvas as the bell sounded.

Zale's seconds, Art Winch and Ray Arcel, told referee Paul Cavalier that their man could not continue. The fight went into the record book as a twelve round knockout. Cerdan was a skillful boxer, unlike Graziano, and Tony had a difficult time penetrating his rugged defense. Add to that, Cerdan could really take a punch.

But Cerdan's tenure as champion was brief. He lost the title in a controversial bout with Jake LaMotta and then died in an airplane crash in the Azores in October of 1949.

Tony told me that painful bone chips in his right elbow had played a role in his loss. His right hand, he said, had no power. At thirty-five Zale hung up the gloves. He stayed in Chicago coaching the CYO boxing team. Although retired Zale was in great shape, keeping his weight in the one hundred and sixty to one hundred and sixty-five pound range.

Then came an ill fated venture. Zale opened a restaurant on Rush Street, on Chicago's glitter gulch but it went under, taking much of Tony's bankroll with it. Zale moved to New York where he served as a greeter at Gallagher's, a well known steakhouse that catered to the sporting crowd.

Zale was slated to get a hefty paycheck of fifteen hundred dollars a week to play himself in *Somebody Up There Likes Me*, a film about Graziano. Zale didn't have to learn any lines, just spar with Paul Newman, who was playing Rocky.

As Rocky explained in his book, by the same name, "All you gotta do is fight natural but pull your punches." Zale was warned by the director to take it easy with Newman because if he didn't he could hurt the star real bad. But when the bell sounded Tony could never take it easy. He staggered Newman and decked the star with a right to the stomach. That was it. Zale blew some easy money and he was out of the picture. MGM got somebody else to play Zale.

The former champion's fortunes though, took a turn for the better in 1970 when he married Philomena "Frisco" Gianfranciso. Philomena, his second wife, had played in the old All Girls Professional Baseball League. The 1940s era league had inspired the movie, *A League Of their Own*.

Philomena felt strongly that her husband had been short changed when it came to capitalizing on his fame. She set out to change that. Philomena hustled his promotional experiences making sure that Tony got a few bucks for his efforts.

She admitted to me that it bothered her that "Peck's bad boy," Graziano, had become a media darling while her straight laced husband, who lived by the golden rule, struggled to make ends meet. Zale, on the other hand, never said he was bitter about his longtime ring rivals, Graziano and Jake LaMotta, making it big in show business.

But there are some things that can't be measured by financial success. In his sunset years Zale worked as a boxing instructor for the Chicago Park District. The pay wasn't great but Tony felt he was helping out youngsters who otherwise might get into trouble. That was a time when Ed Kelly was the park district boss. Ed was a strong boxing supporter who felt Tony could have some influence on teenagers.

As Tony put it, "Basically I teach them to live right which is the most important thing in life anyway." In the 1978 interview at Zale's south side apartment Philomena chimed in, "There are hundreds of young out there who can come back and say if it weren't for Tony Zale I would have gone the wrong way. I would not be the person I am today."

But after sixteen years of working with underprivileged children Tony, who was able to handle blockbuster punches from his opponents was TKO'd by his new bosses at the park district. Zale was terminated from his $15,000 a year job as a consultant. It may have been called a cost cutting move but it was a low blow as far as the Zales were concerned. I recall interviewing the couple in December, 1986, shortly after Tony had been let go. It was obvious that the loss of his job had left the former champion in the doldrums.

In 1990, though, Zale was a headliner one more time. On the fiftieth anniversary of his championship Tony was honored by friends and fans at a big get together on Chicago's near northside. Tony was toasted for his ring skills and bulldog determination. It brought back a lot of great memories and for Tony it was an affair he would never forget. For one more time the Gary native had his moment in the sun.

Two years later tragedy struck the Zale household. His wife Philomena, his protector, publicist, promoter, chauffeur, and best pal died.

Tony's health had also been deteriorating and soon he was suffering from both Parkinson's and Alzheimer's disease. He ended up in a nursing home in Portage, Indiana, where he was diagnosed with lymph node cancer. The end came in March, 1997, when Zale passed away peacefully with his two nieces at his bedside. Zale, who was eighty-three, was survived by his two daughters.

In the late 1950s Zale was contemplating a comeback. The former champion felt the one hundred and sixty pound class was devoid of any real talent with the exception of Sugar Ray Robinson. Zale always kept in tip top shape and believed he could handle the likes of Paul Pender and Gene Fullmer and other top middleweights with ease. Tony wanted a shot at Robinson but despite some ballyhoo about the proposed fight, it never came off. It was just as well. Granted Zale was in great shape for a forty-five year old but he hadn't had a fight in eleven years and would have been no match for Robinson.

How would Zale rank with other one hundred and sixty pound greats?

The late Nat Fleischer, the founder of *Ring* magazine, and a well respected boxing expert, did not have Tony listed in his top ten middleweights of all time.

Nat, in a phone interview with this writer in 1970, admitted that he favored the old timers who fought in the early part of the Twentieth Century. Later, after Fleischer had passed from the scene, a group of editors at the magazine ranked Zale as the seventh best middleweight of all time.

Those not in the Zale camp will say that the Hoosier did not meet the top middleweights of his era such as Ray Robinson, Jake LaMotta, or Charley Burley. That was not Tony's fault. He was in the service for four years and when he got out, Graziano was a promoters' dream, a fighter who could draw a huge gate.

How Zale would fare against other all time greats is a matter of conjecture. But Zale has one record that other boxing immortals can't match. Tony's July, 1940, fight with journeyman Billy Pryor in Milwaukee set a record for attendance that still stands today. One hundred and thirty-five thousand fans saw the bout on Milwaukee's lakefront. There was no admission charge for the fight which was sponsored by the Fraternal Order of Eagles. Zale won by a kayo in the ninth round.

In his prime Tony was as hard a hitter as there was. Billy Soose, who was one of the few titleholders to graduate from college, paid Zale the ultimate compliment. Billy, a graduate of Penn State, scored a close decision over Zale in 1940. But Soose described Tony's body shots as, "Like getting a hot poker stuck in your ribs."

According to newspaper accounts, Zale compiled a record of 70 wins in 88 pro bouts, 46 of those wins coming via the kayo route. He lost 16 fights, most of those defeats occurred early in his career.

Tony was a good one, not the best, probably not in the league with Stanley Ketchel, Harry Greb, or Ray Robinson. However, when it came to guts and determination to get the job done, there was no one better than Tony Zale.

7

THE RED HUNTER

The Daily Worker called him "America's Number One Nazi," Harry Truman sent him one of his famous letters, and *The New York Post* pictured him as a sadist.

He was Harold Velde, a Congressman from central Illinois, who at one time headed the controversial House Un-American Activities Committee during the early 1950s. The Committee became known by its acronym HUAC.

Congressman Harold Velde headed HUAC in the early 1950s.

Velde, in his youth, was a farm boy in the Pekin, Illinois area. He washed dishes to help pay his way through Northwestern University. That led to a teaching and coaching job at the Hillsdale, Illinois high school during the heart of the Depression. But Velde became restless and soon gave law school a shot. He got his law degree from the University of Illinois in 1937. He became an FBI agent during the war and went into politics after V-J Day.

I met Harold Velde at the Dirksen Federal Building in Chicago when Velde was then the regional counsel of the General Services Administration, the business arm of the federal government. He consented one day to a lengthy interview which aired as a two part series on Velde on Channel Two in March, 1971.

Velde said he had a long interest in politics and it was no surprise that he became a county judge in Tazwell County. That neck of the woods was a bastion in the Republican arsenal. Then in 1948, the same year that Truman upset Dewey, Velde was elected to Congress from what is now the 18th Congressional District. Velde made communism the major issue in the campaign. His slogan was "Get the Reds Out of Washington, and Get Washington Out of the Red." Despite being charged as a "red baiter" the former farm boy from Pekin won by a margin of 4,700 votes. Once in Congress Velde asked for and was seated on HUAC, a not too popular place on the hill in those days.

When freshman Congressman Velde arrived on Capitol Hill, HUAC had taken its lumps from critics who decried what they called smear tactics by the Committee.

In the late 1940s the Committee had targeted the entertainment industry, particularly Hollywood. A rash of stars, writers, producers, and executives appeared before the committee. Some were cited for contempt when they refused to answer HUAC questions. The so-called "Hollywood Ten," a group of screen writers, tried to portray themselves as martyrs when they clashed with the Committee.

There was little or no television in 1947, but motion picture newsreels had a field day running highlights of the hearings. Then with flashbulbs popping and klieg lights blazing and with some 300 reporters listening intently the hearings began. And there was plenty of action. The witnesses began insulting the Committee and Committee members fired back insulting the witnesses. It was great theater. The "Hollywood Ten" were or had been members of the Communist Party. The Committee cited the "Hollywood Ten" for contempt and eventually the ten witnesses went to jail. They were cited for contempt, not because of their party affiliation but because they had refused to answer the lawmaker's questions.

Then in 1948 HUAC, which had been getting its share of brickbats for what some called "witch hunts," hit paydirt. It was the Alger Hiss case. Hiss, a former State Department official, had been named a communist by a senior writer at *Time* magazine by the name of Whittaker Chambers. Hiss strongly denied it to his dying day. Their confrontation at a HUAC hearing attracted national attention and was the biggest story of the summer of 1948. Mainly because of the Hiss-Chambers imbroglio, HUAC was saved from extinction. Hiss was later convicted of perjury for lying when he denied passing secret documents to Chambers. He did time at the federal prison in Lewisburg, Pennsylvania.

The Hiss case proved to be a springboard for a freshman congressman from California by the name of Richard Milhous Nixon. Nixon parlayed the Hiss issue into a Senate seat in 1950 when he defeated the incumbent Helen Gahagan Douglas in a rough and tumble campaign. From there it was a path to the White House which Nixon garnered after defeating Hubert Humphrey in 1968.

Thus, when Velde became a Committee member in 1949, HUAC was probably in its heyday. True, a former Committee Chairman, Parnell Thomas, had gone to jail and the press in Washington, by and large, continued to take a dim view of HUAC.

But in 1949 the Cold War was in high gear and Reds in government was becoming a hot issue. Velde got into action in his first term when he got up on the floor of the House and accused President Truman and former President Roosevelt of having a disgraceful security record. Velde urged Congress to investigate the government's security program. Reaction to those remarks was pretty much along party lines. Apparently it didn't hurt him with the folks back home in the heartland. He was unopposed in the GOP primary and won the 1950 general election by a margin of 27,000 votes.

Remember the Korean War was in full force that fall and the fear of Chinese intervention was seen as a very real possibility. The Reds in government issue was a big factor in many of the Congressional campaigns in 1950 and anti-communist candidates came out well in that November election. Some long time Senators bit the dust that year including Democratic powerhouse Scott Lucas of Illinois who was upset by a relatively unknown Everett Dirksen.

During our lengthy interview in 1971 Velde said his experience as an FBI agent working in the bureau's sabotage and counter espionage division alerted him to the dangers of communism. That's one more reason, he said, that he sought a seat on HUAC despite warnings from other politicians that it would hurt his career.

So, Velde in 1949 joined the Committee, then headed by John Wood, a Georgia Democrat. But by then the bloom was starting to come off the rose. Although the Committee got some kudos when it cracked down on the United Electrical, Radio, and Machine Workers Union which was considered under communist influence at that time, HUAC didn't hit any home runs as they did in the Hiss case.

By 1950 HUAC had begun to take a back seat to other Red hunters, such as Senator Joe McCarthy of Wisconsin. McCarthy, a junior senator and an unknown nationally, made a name for himself in a Lincoln Day speech in Wheeling, West Virginia. Joe reportedly said there were 205 communists in the State Department. McCarthy later claimed he said there were 57 communists or security risks in the State Department.

Whatever the figure, the Wheeling speech launched McCarthy as an anti-communist crusader.

Then there was Senator Pat McCarran, the veteran democrat from Nevada. McCarran, a colorful character, headed the Senate Internal Sub-Committee and competed with McCarthy for headlines in the early 1950s. That was shortly after Velde had arrived on the Congressional scene. So HUAC was no longer the happy hunting grounds for an anti-communist. McCarthy and McCarran took over the spotlight. If HUAC had lost some of its luster it wasn't the fault of Velde. In November of 1952, Dwight Eisenhower became President and the GOP captured both houses of Congress. With the Republicans in command Velde became the Chairman of HUAC.

Although HUAC didn't get the headlines its congressional rivals did, Velde didn't let the grass grow under his feet. He had a subpoena issued for former President Harry Truman. Truman ignored the subpoena and blasted Velde verbally in the process. Critics of Velde called the subpoena a publicity stunt and no action was ever taken against Truman for refusing to comply with the subpoena. Truman never appeared before the Committee and no sanctions were issued against the former chief executive.

Velde wanted Truman to explain why he had not fired Harry Dexter White, a key Treasury Department official, when the Justice Department had proof that he had been a Soviet spy.

Truman allegedly had no knowledge of the Justice Department investigation of White and recommended him as head of the International Monetary Fund. The Venona decrypts later revealed that White indeed was a Russian spy, but by the time White's role with the Russians became public the former Treasury Department official had been dead for some time from a heart attack.

The Truman subpoena though, caused some headaches for Velde. Critics claimed he was showboating, desperately trying to keep up with his anti-communist rivals, McCarthy and McCarran. Velde always disputed this, claiming Truman's security program for government employees was sloppy and that the Truman record in this area should have been exposed.

Velde also turned the spotlight on the entertainment industry. In the 1940s the Committee had investigated Reds in Hollywood. That investigation got big play in the media. The Committee did haul a number of celebrities to Washington. Among them was bandleader Artie Shaw, who told the lawmakers that he had been duped by the commies. Velde also subpoenaed some actors but they weren't headliners and the investigation didn't cause much of a ripple. Velde got lot of heat from civil libertarians when he investigated communist influence in universities. And he aroused the ire of liberals when he was quoted as saying, "It's a lot better to wrongly accuse one person of being a Communist than to allow so many to get away with such communist acts as those that have brought us to the brink of World War III."

Velde said he had no regrets about his role with HUAC. He argued that he was focused on rooting out subversives and not on smearing innocent people. Velde's opponents, on the other hand, contended he was a headline grabber more interested in promoting his own agenda rather than exposing actual subversives.

At any rate Velde bowed out. He did not run for re-election but the 18th district he represented remained a Republican bastion. In fact, he was succeeded by his one time administrative assistant Robert Michel, who served many years in Congress.

Velde eventually retired from the government and moved to Arizona, where he died on September 1, 1985. at the age of 75. As for HUAC, it changed its name to the House Internal Security Committee but its stay was short lived. By then Red hunting had fallen in disfavor and the Committee was abolished in 1975.

I DON'T TAKE LIP FROM ANY HOODLUM

Frank Pape, the toughest cop in Chicago. He killed six bad guys. WBBM-TV photo.

Frank Pape hailed from an era when plainclothes detectives wore fedoras and were garbed in Robert Hall or Richman Brothers suits. There were no Miranda warnings then and the good guys didn't wear bulletproof vests.

Pape was a no holds barred robbery detective who earned his stripes with nearly 40 years on the streets of Chicago. And when he retired some 1200 people came to pay tribute to him at a southwest suburban banquet hall. In fact, in an interview with *The Chicago Tribune* in 1994, Phil Cline, then with the Gang Crimes Unit, described Pape as the Babe Ruth of the Police department. Cline later went on to become the Superintendent of Police.

Frank Pape came out of the Bucktown neighborhood on Chicago's near northwest side. Frank's mother and father divorced when the future robbery detective was nine so he, along with his older sister, was raised by his mother. The family didn't have much, so Frank had to drop out of Lane Technical High School to earn some money. Fortunately Frank had an uncle who had a little clout. The uncle was able to get the youngster into the Sheet Metal Workers Union as an apprentice.

It appeared that young Pape was set for life. He passed the apprentice examination and went to trade school so he could become a full fledged sheet metal worker. The pay was good, there was plenty of work available, and Frank's career was pretty well set. For seven years Pape toiled in the sheet metal trade but then came Black Friday and the Depression. All bets were off. Trade jobs were tough to get and his uncle didn't have the kind of clout to get him any work. So Pape began to look elsewhere.

Then another uncle of Pape got into the act. He suggested that Pape try his hand at becoming a Chicago firefighter. That suggestion made a lot of sense to the young ex-sheet metal worker. A firefighter position meant good pay and lifetime security, a real bonus in the Depression era. Besides, Frank liked to help people, and as a firefighter he would be doing just that. But there was one fly in the ointment. The Fire Department had canceled its plans for an examination that year. It appeared that Pape's hopes to work for the city had gone down the drain. However, a civil service clerk told Pape that the police department was hiring, so the Bucktown resident decided to give that a shot.

In that era, the 1930s, most cops fit the old flatfoot image—big heavy-set, six footers. That was something Pape was not. In those days the department's height and weight minimums were more stringent than they are today. Pape was underweight by department standards but once he had his mind set there was no turning back.

Chuck Adamson, a former Chicago policeman and now a Hollywood screen writer, penned a book about Pape in 2001 called appropriately enough *The Toughest Cop In America.* We interviewed Adamson a couple of years ago and he explained what Pape did in order to be eligible to take the police exam. "Frank was 5′ 10″ at that time and weighed about 147 pounds. The physical exam required the applicant to expand his chest 3 inches and flex his muscles. Well, he didn't really have a big girth and he needed to put on a few pounds. And in order to do that he ate a whole bunch of bananas and drank a lot of water."

Those bananas paid off and Pape put on the necessary weight to pass his physical. The minimum at that time was 150 pounds and Frank barely made it. So in 1933 Pape joined the Police Department as a patrolman. Pape's first assignment was at the Albany Park district on the northwest side. There he pounded a beat and learned like all good cops to twirl his baton. Pape wasn't there very long before he was assigned to the States Attorney's office to work on gambling and prostitution. Although that assignment was temporary duty he caught the eye of some veteran detectives who liked his approach. Soon Pape was back in Albany Park, but this time in plainclothes.

Author Adamson said Pape had an uncanny ability to spot potential trouble waiting to happen. It was woe to the hoodlum who would take liberties with honest citizens. Adamson related to me that Pape once told him, "The people of Chicago have the right to be secure in their homes. They have the right to walk the streets in peace and to use the parks if they choose without being molested. If someone chooses to bother them, then they're going to have to reckon with me."

It wasn't long before Pape got a reputation as a no non-sense cop. He was quoted in one national magazine as saying, "I'm not going to take any lip from a hoodlum." Long after he had retired, Pape told me his philosophy, "With me, its dog eat dog. If you shoot at me I'm going to kill you if I can. I'm not going along with this kind of business of taking those kinds of guys alive. I don't believe in it and I don't care if I'm criticized for it or not." Remember, Pape was in his heyday in the 1940s and 1950s. His free wheeling style would raise a hailstorm of criticism in this era.

Actually Pape recalled that he never fired a gun at a criminal in his first 12 years on the force. That all changed in the summer of 1945 when his partner Morris Friedman, a veteran detective, was shot and killed in a shootout. Friedman's philosophy was to fire a warning shot before trying to shoot to injure or kill someone. But in this instance the felon, an ex-con from Detroit shot back hitting and mortally wounding Friedman. The ex-con in turn was shot to death by another Chicago detective.

The death of Friedman stuck in Frank's craw and from then on Pape would shoot first and ask questions later.

Several months after Friedman's death, Pape was in a take no prisoners mood. He and his partner were involved in a shootout near Milwaukee Avenue. According to reports, one of the gunmen had emptied his revolver at Pape in a futile attempt to hit the policeman. Out of ammunition the gunman offered to surrender, but Pape settled his case out of court and gunned down his opponent, killing him instantly. Pape's actions as an executioner would have netted him at least a suspension and probably a dismissal from the force if the incident had been reported in this day and age. Probably if the deceased had any relatives, a huge lawsuit would be filed against the city.

But that was in 1945 and the majority of the public supported Pape and so did the department. Pape, himself, never had any qualms of conscience about the incident, or for that matter, similar affairs when criminals were gunned down. As he told me in a 1979 interview, "I never shot a man who didn't have a gun in his hand. Those things never bothered me and I'm sure it never will. And I didn't mince any words or actions with a guy who had a gun in his hand." And then Pape repeated his Darwinian view of survival, "I think it was just dog eat dog and kill or be killed."

Soon Pape had gotten a tough guy reputation in underworld circles. As the story goes, when Pape's squad car would show up, hoodlums would soon clear out. Before long he was running the robbery detail and had been promoted to Captain. The national media loved him and Pape was featured in close to 50 stories in various detective-type magazines which were very popular in the 1950s.

As Pape's legend grew so did stories about him. He was involved in at least 16 shoot-outs although author Adamson says it was 23. How many men did he kill? Most sources say he gunned down nine offenders. When I asked Pape how many criminals he had slain, he replied, "I won't talk about it." Then Pape looked down at a revolver he was holding and said, "This gun killed six."

It was no wonder that the flamboyant Pape's name surfaced when the department began a nationwide search in 1960 for a new superintendent. The department had been rocked by a major scandal when some officers at a north side district had allied themselves with a professional burglar. The crooked cops soon became known as the "Burglars in Blue." Their tales of police villainy become the fodder for television and night club comics. The burglar, Richard Morrsion, was called the "Babbling Burglar" after he exposed the cops' role in the breaking and entering scheme.

Morrison cased a number of north side stores, then burglarized them as the rogue cops acted as lookouts. Then the cops moved in and loaded their cars with stolen merchandise. Eight of the cops were arrested and convicted. Five did time in the Big House, one did a short stint in the county jail, and two were fined and placed on probation.

With the nation having a field day poking fun at the police department, Mayor Daley was under pressure to find a reformer who would ferret out any corruption. Although Pape couldn't have been considered a reform candidate, he had been promoted to Deputy Chief of Detectives in 1957 and he had plenty of support. Frank had the ear of the mayor who admired the veteran robbery detective. But it wasn't to be.

Daley reached out to the west coast and selected the University of California's Dean of Criminology, Orlando Wilson, for the task of shaping up the department. Reportedly, two high ranking police officers did not like Pape and had been bad mouthing him. How much influence these men had with Pape not getting the top job is speculation. But their efforts certainly didn't help Pape's cause. And there was also the matter of an $8,000 judgment a jury had ordered Pape to pay. The jury had found that Pape had violated the civil rights of a murder suspect. Add to this, some citizens were becoming sharply critical of Pape's aggressive style.

With Wilson taking over as superintendent in 1960, Pape began to look elsewhere for greener pastures. At least one prominent businessman tried to convince Frank to run for Cook County Sheriff. He wasn't interested.

In 1961, Pape took a leave of absence to head up security at Arlington Park, the crown jewel of Illinois racetracks. He also was in charge of security of Washington Park, another racetrack operated by Marge Everett. Racetrack officials were growing concerned about syndicate bookmakers and Outfit juice loan thugs hanging out at area tracks. Pape knew a lot of mob guys on sight, ranging from soldiers to bosses like Tony

Accardo, so he was the ideal choice to keep out mobsters who frequented racetracks.

But after four years at the tracks Pape did not renew his leave of absence with the department. He came back to active duty with the force. That was in 1965 and the "Brass" couldn't decide where to assign their highly publicized colleague. Eventually he headed up the Traffic Division. That's where Pape wound up his career, retiring in 1972.

So suburban Park Ridge was where he spent his sunset years. I recall visiting Pape several times at his home and remember that Winnebago parked in the driveway. He and his wife, Kitty, got their mileage out of that recreational vehicle, taking off on various trips around the country

It was on one of those visits to Park Ridge that I questioned Pape about the deterrent value of capital punishment. That really set Frank off. Frank felt very strongly about that subject. He put it this way, "It certainly has a deterrent value. We got all these kind of self-styled experts who say it has no deterrent value. They don't know what they are talking about because I've talked to guys who went to the chair. I've talked to guys before they went there so I know what the value of it is. And society today, you know, they don't exact their pound of flesh as they should."

Pape contended he had seen convicted felons make deals with the State's Attorney and spill their beans about their confederates in an effort to avoid the death penalty.

The term legend is vastly overused these days. Journeyman athletes, news people, politicians, generals, and civil servants became legends simply because they stuck around so long. In Pape's case, he was a real legend whose exploits were well known beyond Chicago's borders. But even legends are human and they, like all of us, have human frailties. Frank Pape died in March of 2000. He was 91 years old.

Could Frank's shoot first and ask questions later style cut it in this day and age? As author Adamson summed it up. "It would be pretty difficult for Frank to exist today. Not because he was not adaptable to new rules, regulations, and social attitudes. But Frank was Frank. He felt he knew what he did was in the best interests of law enforcement and what was in the best interests for the citizens of Chicago. And he would let the chips fall as they may."

9

THE REWARD

For 20 years Leon Falcon has been on a personal crusade to find out who was responsible for the deaths of two of his friends, Donna Lynn Hartwell and Frank Matous. Hartwell was more than a friend to Leon. In fact Donna was the love of Leon's life.

Matous, who authorities referred to as a minor drug figure, was found shot to death in the trunk of a burned out car

Frank Matous, slain in McHenry County. Leon Falcon photo.

Leon Falcon and Donna Hartwell. Falcon has been on a crusade to find Donna's killer. Leon Falcon photo.

in Algonquin, a community in McHenry County. The next day, September 5, 1987, River Grove Police discovered the body of Donna Hartwell in Matous' apartment in that western suburb. Hartwell, who was estranged from her husband, was the mother of a little girl and Falcon said Hartwell was staying with Matous temporarily The Cook County Medical Examiner's Office ruled that Hartwell's death was the result of a massive cocaine overdose. Falcon said Donna "had enough drugs in her to kill a thoroughbred." There were marks on Hartwell's neck and some investigators theorized that Hartwell was killed because she had either witnessed Matous's murder or knew who did it. Falcon is convinced that the overdose was induced by Matous's killers.

The death of Donna became an obsession to Falcon. According to Leon, he and Donna were planning to be married as soon as their divorces from their respective spouses became final. Falcon first saw Donna at a neighbor's cookout in 1979 but it wasn't until 1983 that they began dating and fell in love. Donna became pregnant but a miscarriage ended the couple's hope for a daughter.

Falcon was born light years away from Chicago in the Texas border town of Del Rio. The family moved to Chicago when Leon was five years old and the youngster went to parochial grade school and graduated from Wells High School. Leon tried his hand at various enterprises as he reached middle age. He operated a store for precious metals and then for a longer time (1972-83) ran a motorcycle shop on Chicago's west side. It was there that he became acquainted with Matous, an avid biker.

The deaths though of Hartwell and Matous changed Falcon's life. He opened a tavern on the northwest side, calling it Donna and Frank's Unicorn 10 Pub, in memory of his late friends. The walls of the tavern were plastered with photos of Donna and Frank, as well as reward posters asking for information about the case. Falcon, an Elvis Presley fan, also filled the tavern with Presley memorabilia.

Falcon felt that authorities needed a boost to their investigation and decided to post a $50,000 reward for information leading to the arrest and conviction of Matous's and Hartwell's killers. Those with information were urged to call the McHenry County Sheriff's Police, the River Grove Police department, or Crime Stoppers.

$50,000 was a substantial figure for Falcon to pony up. So he held a fund raiser at the tavern which garnered about $10,000. Falcon then re-mortgaged his Chicago home to make up the difference. He later sold the tavern and is now in the retail business. Leon said if he had the financial resources he would raise the reward to one million dollars.

Ironically, for a time Falcon was himself a suspect in the murders. Detectives theorized there had been a love triangle between Falcon, Matous, and Hartwell, and that Leon, jealous of Matous's attention to Donna, killed them both. Falcon was later able to convince investigators that he had nothing to do with the two deaths.

Falcon has been doing some sleuthing on his own, becoming a one man detective agency as far as the case in concerned. Leon believes that a person doing time in a downstate penitentiary can shed some light on the mystery. Falcon says he volunteered to wear a concealed body recorder while interviewing the prisoner in the jail. But according to Leon, the McHenry County Sheriffs Department nixed the offer, saying it would be too dangerous. Falcon feels the actual killer is someone else, someone he says is now out of an Illinois prison.

Despite the fact that the reward money has failed to provide any substantial leads on the case, Falcon is still optimistic that the murders will be solved and the killer or killers will brought to justice. Falcon concedes that he is obsessed about the case and he says his love for Donna is still as strong as it

Headstone of Donna Lynn Hartwell-Kostrezeski, the love of Leon's life. Leon Falcon photo.

was twenty years ago. Donna was 17 years Leon's junior, but that Falcon says never interfered with their relationship.

Although Hartwell has been dead for about twenty years Falcon makes weekly pilgrimages to her grave in south suburban Homewood's Memorial Garden Cemetery. According to Falcon he bought the marble tombstone which has an inscription, "I Love You." Leon has a plot next to Donna's grave.

I did a story about Falcon and his reward in 1990 and he appears just as determined now as he did then to see to it that the killer or killers are caught and punished. As he munched a BLT in a north suburban restaurant, years after the slayings, he brandished a thick photo album containing pictures and memorabilia of Hartwell. He has sent letters or contacted network or syndicated news show hoping they would do a story on Donna and Frank Matous. Those shows include *Unsolved Mysteries* and *48 Hours*, among others.

He has also written an unpublished manuscript entitled *The Ultimate Dream*, a story of his love for Hartwell who he describes as the "Beautifulist [sic] and most gorgeous woman in the world." Falcon says even if the reward fails to provide any viable information about the mystery, he doesn't intend to throw in the towel. As Leon puts it, "I'll never give up until justice is done."

10

HARD LINERS

George Lincoln Rockwell and Robert DePugh got their share of ink in the 1960s warning their followers that Armageddon was near. Rockwell, a national figure, died violently in 1967. He was the founder of the American Nationalist Socialist Party or American Nazi Party, as it was more commonly known. DePugh was the founder of the Minuteman, a militant anti-communist organization. We'll have more to say on DePugh later.

Rockwell, an Ivy Leaguer, could put on quite a charm act, when he wanted to. When I was working at WHO in Des Moines, Iowa, I spent half an hour interviewing Rockwell. Before the interview, which was held in the WHO studios, Rockwell politely inquired as to where he could get his suit cleaned. Then after briefly discussing his education and military background Rockwell warned me that once the camera light came on his personality would change. In other words, a lot of that ranting and raving was an act that he used to impress his followers and possibly convert some TV viewers into joining the party. Not that he didn't believe the stuff he was talking about, but his views were not as unalterable as his public persona would indicate.

In some ways Rockwell reminded me of some pro wrestlers that I had interviewed. They too had to project a tough guy image when the camera light was on and their actions

George Lincoln Rockwell (man with pipe), American Nazi leader, with Drummond. WHO-TV photo.

were being recorded. The only difference was that the grapplers didn't espouse racial hatred, something Rockwell would do once he got going.

Rockwell's roots were in the Midwest. He was born in Bloomington, Illinois, in 1918 and then spent his youth on the east coast after his parents were divorced. There was nothing to indicate in his early years his hatred of some minorities. He went to boarding school in Maine, and attended Brown University, hardly a hotbed of extreme right wingers. His fellow students remember Rockwell as taking conservative positions in debates with his more liberal colleagues, but his positions on social issues were not extreme at all.

He dropped out of Brown before the war to join the Navy. There he went to flight school and became a pilot and was given credit for helping sink two German U-boats off the African coast. After V-J Day Rockwell, by then a married man, went to the Pratt Institute in Brooklyn hoping to become a commercial artist.

It was there, in the melting pot that was New York City that Rockwell took notice of people of mixed racial heritage. It was there that Rockwell formed his racial views that were to play a major role in his life.

But he didn't develop a serious interest in politics until 1950 when the Korean War broke out. The Navy called him back to active duty as a Lt. Commander and assigned him to an installation in San Diego where he trained Navy pilots in close air support. The naval rank of Commander would stick with Rockwell for the rest of his life even when he was released from active duty. His subordinates in Des Moines, I recall, would refer to him as Commander Rockwell when he was being addressed.

His second tour of Navy duty apparently turned him into a political extremist. It was an era when anti-communist fever was running high. Red hunters like Senator Joe McCarthy, Senator Pat McCarran, and Representative Harold Velde were grabbing headlines. The Red Chinese had intervened in Korea and it appeared that World War III was a strong possibility. There was talk that a communist conspiracy had sold out China to the Reds, and anti-Semites like Gerald K. Smith were warning that the Jews were behind the communist conspiracy.

Rockwell, in 1952, was re-assigned to a post in Iceland. There in the capital of Reykjavik he met a "Nordic beauty," Thora Haligrimsson, who would become his second wife. He was divorced by his first wife by then. Their honeymoon was spent at Berchtesgaden near where Hitler had his famed mountain retreat, the Eagle's Nest.

Upon his discharge from the Navy Rockwell, no longer interested in art as a vocation, switched gears and started a couple of publishing ventures. These publications, although not successful financially, gave Rockwell an opportunity to voice his views on racial integration and communism. During this period he worked for a time at *The National Review*, a conservative magazine, launched by the colorful William F.

Buckley. However, Rockwell later felt that readers of publications like *The National Review* were "human ostriches" who hid their heads in the sand rather than take a strong stand against communism and other dangers.

Ironically, Minuteman head Robert DePugh felt the same way about Rockwell and his band. That is, according to DePugh, the Rockwell crowd wasn't much more than a debating society only willing to talk about real issues rather taking action.

In 1955, Rockwell went off the deep end and ended any semblance of political moderation. He called it "crossing the Rubicon." In July of that year he picketed in front of the White House with a sign that read "Save Ike from the kikes." He was opposed to an administration decision to send Marines to Lebanon and save a regime that had been considered pro-Israeli.

It wasn't long after that Rockwell became a national figure. He founded the American Nazi Party in 1959, with headquarters in Arlington, Virginia. He had several publications, pamphlets, or newspapers espousing Nazi views and he urged young men 18 and over to become Storm Troopers. The would-be Storm Troopers had to be of the right racial and ethnic origins.

In the early 1960s Rockwell had established party branches in several major cities, including Chicago. It was in Chicago in 1966 that Rockwell led a counter demonstration in Cicero opposing Dr. Martin Luther King's attempt to end de facto segregation in that suburb. Then a year later, Rockwell changed the name of the American Nazi Party to the National Socialist White People's Party.

By then Rockwell had become quite a draw on college campuses. It was good way to help the party coffers and perhaps draw a few converts. Many of the students who heard Rockwell's lectures were there out of curiosity, some were there to boo and jeer Rockwell, while a few showed up because they identified their views with the Nazi leader.

When we interviewed Rockwell in Des Moines, he was in the Iowa capital to give a lecture at Drake University. In that interview we asked Rockwell if he feared he would be assassinated. Rockwell claimed he was not fearful of being assassinated although he admitted it was a possibility. He said some Jew or "Commie" might try to kill him but he said his own men were most always on hand to protect him. When we did our interview with Rockwell I noticed he had two of his Storm Troopers with him acting as bodyguards.

There were no bodyguards or Storm Troopers with him on August 25, 1967. That's when Rockwell had just dropped off his clothes at a laundromat in Arlington, Virginia. A sniper, perched on the roof of the shopping mall where the laundromat was located, fired at least two shots at the Nazi leader. Rockwell was killed almost instantly.

The assassin was not a communist, a left winger, a Jew, or a black man. The killer was a member of Rockwell's party. The shooter was identified as one John Patler, a captain in the American Nazi Party. In explaining why Patler shot the American "Fuhrer," Matt Koehl, who succeeded Rockwell, said Patler had been expelled from the party because he had what Koehl described as "Bolshevik leanings."

With the death of Rockwell the movement lost steam. He was charismatic and was able to attract followers that his successors could not do to that degree. As for Rockwell, had he not gone the rabble rouser route with his violent hatred of minorities, he could have played a role on the political scene. He was good looking, an excellent speaker, a war hero, and had an Ivy League education. Yet, instead he chose to throw away a possibly bright career by espousing views that were morally repugnant to most Americans. In our interview Rockwell's strong support of Adolph Hitler came at a time when memories of the war and Nazi atrocities were all too fresh. Had he played his cards differently Rockwell could have won support from a number of citizens rather than a small hard core minority.

Rockwell's party faded from the headlines after his death until another rabble rouser played the media for all it was worth in Chicago. That was Frank Collin, the Chicago "Fuhrer." Collin, while attending Southern Illinois University in 1963, became attracted to the American Nazi Party after reading the writings of Rockwell. He joined the party in 1965 and shortly after met Rockwell. That was a magic moment for him. Colin returned to Chicago and devoted all his energies to furthering the cause of Nazism.

In one of his earlier acts, Collin broke away from the old Rockwell group in Arlington, Virginia, and formed a new organization called the National Socialist Party of America. He claimed the Arlington, Virginia, group had deviated from the program of it's founder George Lincoln Rockwell. Don't get the idea that Collin was soft pedaling the Hitlerian line. He continued to preach hatred for Jews, blacks and communists.

Collin set up shop in what was then party headquarters on 71st Street in the Marquette Park area on the city's southwest side. Collin devoted all his energies to the Nazi cause, actually living in the building which was called Rockwell Hall.

 He soon claimed that he had the largest Nazi chapter in the country. Give the devil his due: Collin knew how to attract media attention. He ran for an aldermanic seat in 1975 and later was a candidate for Congress in the Third Congressional District. Needless to say, he lost both races but he kept his name in the public eye. Then came a stunt that put Collin's name and his party on the map

He announced that he and his Storm Troopers would hold a march and rally in the suburb of Skokie. Skokie in the 1970s was a predominantly Jewish suburb and some of its residents were survivors of World War II Nazi concentration camps.

You can imagine how the proposed Nazi march and rally was going over in Skokie. There was a tremendous hue and cry and city officials went to court to try to block the march.

The story received national media attention and there was even a TV movie made about it, starring Danny Kaye. When the Nazi right to march in Skokie was being debated in the courts, Collin had a field day. News conferences at Rockwell Hall, the Nazi headquarters, became a weekly if not daily occurrence, with Collin holding forth. Collin had no intention of gong to Skokie. It was strictly a ploy to get publicity and also force the Chicago Park District to grant him a permit to hold a rally in the more friendly confines of Marquette Park.

He and his youthful followers also held a rally in downtown Chicago at the Kluczynski Federal Building Plaza. It was not a pleasant outing for the Collin gang. The Storm Troopers were bombarded with eggs and tomatoes tossed by counter demonstrators.

The main event came later on July 9, 1978, when Collin and his henchman got their chance to sell their wares before a crowd which police estimated at more than two thousand. I was impressed that day the way Chicago Police handled the demonstration in what was a volatile situation. The cops were out in mass, some in uniform, some in plainclothes, and others mounted on horseback. They kept the Nazis and counter demonstrators separate and ended up arresting some 72 people. The crowd milled around for a time and then went home. There was no riot.

The demonstration itself was typical of those involving Collin's group. The Storm Troopers, vastly outnumbered by protestors, would shout "anti-Jewish" remarks while the counter demonstrators chanted "anti-Nazi" slogans. It was probably the high water mark for Collin and his group. For Collin it was all downhill after that.

It was revealed in a Chicago newspaper that Frank Collin's father was a German born Jew who survived the concentration camp at Dachau and became a U.S. citizen. Collin's father, who was born Max Simon Cohn, immigrated to this country and married a Roman Catholic and moved to the south suburbs. The father, who changed his name to Collin, was very unhappy that Frank had gone the Nazi route. The elder Collin reportedly asked young Frank to leave home. Frank, at first denied he was half Jewish, but his Nazi colleagues obviously couldn't be taking orders from somebody who was not a pure Aryan.

Then came the body blow that sent Frank to prison. In January of 1979, Collin was arrested by Chicago Police and charged with sexually abusing children. According to authorities, Collin would pick up young boys and take them to Rockwell Hall where he showed them pornographic movies and then had sex with them. In March of 1980 Collin pleaded guilty to taking indecent liberties with five boys who ranged in age from 11 to 15. He was sentenced to seven years in jail.

Collin's notoriety surrounding his child molestation charges gave the Nazis a black eye. Collin had become the most publicized American Nazi since Rockwell and now his one time allies called him not only a Jew, but a fag as well.

With Collin out of the picture, a rival group from the National Socialist White People's Party set up headquarters in Cicero. The group tried to stir up interest by holding several rallies including an ill fated affair in Evanston. The 1980 Evanston rally was held in a park in the northern area of the suburb. The Nazis were met by a big crowd of protestors, estimated at several thousand. The counter demonstrators not only booed the Nazis but showered them with eggs, rocks, and other debris. The Nazis were unable to make their speeches heard and soon beat a hasty retreat with a contingent of law enforcement personnel separating them from the crowd that had gotten ugly.

Since Collin's departure the local Nazi group hasn't had the "pizzazz" of years gone by. The skin head movement has recycled some neo-Nazi groups and the Aryan Nation has attracted some disciples while others have converted to organizations such as Matt Hale's World Church of the Creator. But there haven't been any leaders like Rockwell who had the charisma to attract much of a following.

While Rockwell was barnstorming round the country, talking at college campuses, another right wing organization was attracting the attention of federal authorities. That was the Minutemen, not to be confused with the group that patrols the U. S. border with Mexico in an attempt to stop illegal immigration. The Minutemen I'm referring to was a militant group that feared an impending takeover of the government by communists.

Its leader was Robert DePugh of Norbonne, Missouri, the president of a small veterinary medicine supply firm. The

Robert DePugh, head of the Minutemen, with Drummond. WHO-TV photo.

Minutemen has been organized in secret cells of five to 15 members. The movement had its greatest strength in Missouri and southern Illinois, although it did have chapters in California and in New York state. Many of the members had stockpiled weapons and would train on weekends so that they would be able to defend the U.S. against what members called communists and other subversives.

We did a lengthy interview with DePugh in Des Moines, Iowa, in 1967 when he was in the Iowa capital trying to recruit new members. At the time DePugh was out on bond while appealing a conviction of violating federal firearms laws. One of the charges against the Minutemen leader was that DePugh possessed several automatic weapons, including a 50 caliber machine gun, without paying a firearms tax stamp for the weapons.

DePugh laid his cards on the table during the 30 minute interview which was broadcast over WHO-TV. "We are building an underground army to protect our freedoms, our American heritage against a communist controlled government or a communist takeover." DePugh and his followers believed in playing hard ball.

Several months before our interview nineteen New York Minutemen were arrested and accused of planning to bomb and burn three summer camps in the New York metropolitan area. A large cache of weapons was seized by law enforcement officers including rifles, pipe bombs, mortars, machine guns, a grenade launcher, and a bazooka

DePugh described the camps as being operated by communist front groups that taught Red ideology. He said the camps were "immoral and had a degrading environment." And the Missouri right winger added, "If many people knew those things that were taking place, they would say they deserved to be raided."

The New York Minutemen never did any time despite what the government claimed was overwhelming evidence. Because of faulty search warrants the charges against the Minutemen were finally dropped in 1971.

In 1965, the then Attorney General for the state of California, Thomas Lynch, released an 81 page report that described the Minutemen as a threat to the peace and security of the state. The report went on to say that the Minutemen embraced violent racial and political doctrines. DePugh was nonplussed by attacks on his group, taking verbal salvos at the government brass. "I think there are very high ups in the government, people who would sell us out to the communists, just as fast as they could do so."

And DePugh, during our interview, took pot shots at other right wing groups. He called the John Birch Society, a "debating society," conceding the Birchers had taken an anti-communist line but arguing that Robert Welch's group were talkers who didn't do anything against the "Red Menace." As for Rockwell's Nazi organization, DePugh heaped more disdain. He questioned if Rockwell was a communist himself, claiming the Nazi leader had hurt the anti-communist cause. As to the Rockwell Storm Troopers, DePugh scoffed that they were "just talkers and not do'ers."

However, the Minutemen leader didn't ride high in the saddle for long. A federal grand jury indicted DePugh and seven other Minutemen on charges of conspiring to rob a bank. DePugh went underground and for seventeen months remained on the lam. DePugh's underground sojourn ended when he was apprehended in Truth or Consequences, New Mexico. He was sentenced to prison on a variety of federal charges Barred by terms of his parole DePugh was unable to reactivate the Minutemen following his incarceration. It was not a large group to begin with and the Minutemen were no longer a presence on the radical right scene. Some of DePugh's cadre, though drifted over to other right wing groups.

Another right wing extremist fearing Armageddon is John Harrell, known as "Johnny Bob" to all the folks in and around

John Harrel, right wing extremist, in front of his home, a replica of Mt. Vernon.

downstate Louisville, Illinois. Harrell, a wealthy businessman, who claimed he was cured of lymph cancer after a divine apparition, founded the Christian Conservative Church as well as the Christian Patriots Defense League. He directs the fight against communism from his home, which by the way is a 55 acre estate on which sits a replica of Mt. Vernon—only 20 percent larger than the original.

When I talked to Harrell in 1983 he was concerned that trouble was brewing. "We are now on a collision course with a revolutionary situation. We believe we have now gone to the point of no return. We believe we have polarized the nation to such a degree politically, economically, spiritually, that in our opinion, we are going to move into a revolutionary circumstance that is sweeping the whole world."

But it wasn't Harrell's views that got him into trouble with Uncle Sam. In 1961 federal authorities arrested "Johnny Bob" for harboring a Marine deserter. Harrell spent four years in a federal prison before resuming his anti-communist crusade. After his release from jail, Harrell didn't spend all his time just talking and warning about the dangers of communism.

He set up survival training on his estate grounds where CPDL members could engage in paramilitary war games.

Soon Harrell's property wasn't big enough to play soldier. When we visited Harrell he had moved his survival conference to Licking, Missouri, where there was more land available for his troops. A brochure on the Licking meeting stated that "...only quality patriots were wanted." There at the 232 acre survival base Harrell's followers could train in preparation for the Doomsday they felt was coming.

Harrell claimed members could be of any race or religion as long as they were Christian and a patriot. But he didn't believe in mixing races, saying the impending meeting was for Caucasians only. Harrell's sessions were definitely a mostly white crowd. As for the revolution Harrell told me, "It can occur anytime, the stage is set, all it takes is the catalyst. It can be racial, it can be political, it can be military. There are several ways it can go and when it does, it may spread like a prairie fire." So far Harrell's prophecy of doom and revolution has not borne fruit.

Hundreds of miles from Harrell's home near Louisville, Illinois, is Tigerton Dells, Wisconsin, which in the 1980s served as the Badger state's headquarters for the Posse Comitatus. Tigerton Dells is in northeast Wisconsin and I, along with cameraman Bill Burk and producer Ruth Fitzpatrick, made a pit stop there in connection with a series we were doing for WBBM-TV called "Thunder On The Right."

The Posse Comitatus is an anti-tax and survivalist group that was little known until February, 1983. That all changed when two U. S. Marshals were killed in a Medina, North Dakota, shootout with Gordon Kahl, who said he was the leader of the Posse. Kahl became a fugitive and was later traced to Arkansas where he was killed in anther shootout with lawmen. Kahl became a martyr in the eyes of some Posse members. It was about that time that the Justice Department labeled the Posse as a domestic terrorist group.

The name Posse Comitatus is Latin and it means "power to the people." The Posse believes literally that all government should be rooted at the county level. The group takes a strong stand against the IRS, contending income taxes are unconstitutional. It also argues that an "international Jewish conspiracy" controls the banking industry.

When our pilgrimage took us to the Posse compound, the anti-tax group was holding a rally. Before the rhetoric started we chatted with James Wickstrom, who was billed as the Director of Counterinsurgency for the organization. Wickstrom did not beat around the bush when it came to discussing the federal government and its law enforcement agencies. "The IRS is a terrorist organization. At this time the Anti-Defamation League, the FBI, and the U.S. Marshals are just subjecting the people to terrorism."

The people attending the Posse rally were mostly Wisconsin residents who worked or farmed in the area. They didn't appear to be "kooks" or fanatics, just people looking for answers to everyday problems. They may not have come up with any solutions to their problems but they got some fiery rhetoric from a man identified as Lt. Colonel Gordon "Jack" Mohr, a spokesman for the Christian Patriots Defense League. It was a theme of Armageddon now as Mohr warned his audience of a coming bloodbath. "When is America going to wake up? Are we going to wake up when the Asiatic hordes goosestep down the streets of our city? Are we going to wake up when they come into our homes and rape our wives and daughters and murder our sons? When are we going to open our eyes to the danger that is facing us?"

Inflammatory oratory with racial overtones was the order of the day. Wickstrom, who once ran for Governor of Wisconsin on the Constitution Party's ticket, made that clear when he talked to us. "We don't allow any Jews in. They don't allow us into the Anti-Defamation League or B'nai Brith. We don't want to be a part of a communist organization."

The Posse at that time (1983) claimed to have had two million members. However, law enforcement officials then put the number at less than ten thousand with no more than several hundred hard core members

Groups like the Posse appeal to people who haven't gotten their share of the American dream. Extremist rhetoric can be attractive because it offers simple solutions to compl ex-problems. And there is always a scapegoat. In the case of the Posse it's the Jews and the IRS among others. In bad times extremist rhetoric can find an audience to those seeing their entire way of life disappear, farmers facing foreclosure, factory workers losing their jobs because of new technology, and ordinary citizens fed up with big government.

11

THE NEW DILLINGERS

He was a former seminarian and a respected suburban businessman, while his son, a graduate of Loyola University, was an accountant. To neighbors and business associates the pair, John Hunter, Sr. and John Jr. appeared to be law abiding citizens. But to the FBI this father and son combo were the notorious flesh-masked bandits who terrorized a number of mid-western banks. In fact the father and son team did so well that they made the Dillinger gang and Bonnie and Clyde look like pikers.

The duo got the flesh-masked moniker because of the disguises they used when robbing banks. John Hunter, Sr. often used an opaque latex mask of a smiling old man, while John

John Hunter, Sr. and John Hunter, Jr. befuddled authorities for some time. FBI photos.

Hunter, Jr. often wore a mask purporting to be former Democratic presidential candidate Michael Dukakis.

The Hunters were convicted of robbing 16 banks in suburban Chicago and several other mid-western states. Unlike most of their bank robbing contemporaries in the early 1990s, the father and son duo scored big. Authorities estimate that between May of 1992 and March of 1993, the Hunters garnered over $250,000 in their ten month bank robbery spree.

Most bank robberies nowadays are solo jobs, with the bandit fleeing with chump change of $2,500 or less. That was not the case with the Hunters. Assistant U.S. Attorney Victoria Peters described the Hunters as "very professional, very meticulous, in planning their jobs." Peters said the Hunters kept their target banks under surveillance, checking when employees would come and go and noting the best escape routes. The Hunters acted with military precision leaving little for chance. Their getaway vehicles were usually stolen and most had stolen license plates.

The Hunters were relative newcomers to a life of crime when they robbed their first bank in Wauwatosa, Wisconsin. Authorities believe the pair went off the straight and narrow because of financial problems. The elder Hunter had become an unemployed business consultant and John Jr. had been fired from his job at a north suburban accounting firm. Adding to the younger Hunter's woes, his wife had filed for divorce.

Hunter Sr. had gone solo on several jobs but a badly injured knee prompted him to seek a confederate. That accomplice turned out to be John Jr. who, armed with a gun, got over $3,000 in the duo's first heist together. The elder Hunter drove the getaway car in that score.

Soon the pairs' M.O. gave the Hunters a modicum of fame. The flesh masked bandits were leaving their calling cards all too often. The two were having a field day as they hit one bank after another. Although they were charged with 16 bank robberies investigators believe their total was closer to 35 with as much as $400,000 taken in the heists.

The pair was never apprehended on a bank job but their spree came to an end in April, 1993. That's when an Indiana police officer on routine patrol spotted the elder Hunter changing a license plate at a West Lafayette shopping mall at one o'clock in the morning. When the officer approached John Sr., the elder Hunter jumped into his car and a high speed chase ensued. At one point, a passenger in the Hunter vehicle leaned out the window and began firing at their pursuers. Police believe it was the younger Hunter who fired the shots.

Masked man committing bank robbery (John Hunter, Sr.).

By now more police were joining the chase with the Hunter vehicle hitting speeds of 85 miles per hour. Chased by county, local police, and even a security guard, the chase finally ended when the elder Hunter was apprehended at a farm house. The manhunt concluded the next day when John Jr. was arrested at a restaurant not far from where the chase began. The Hunters did not go down without a fight. One police officer was shot in the leg as several bullets hit his squad car.

Hunter Sr. had an explanation for his bizarre behavior. John Sr. said he did not know it was a police officer who confronted him in a parking lot. According to the elder Hunter, he thought he was being targeted for a robbery so he fled the scene. As to the number of weapons found in his vehicle, the father had an explanation. He told authorities he and his son were heading to Louisville, Kentucky, where they were going to compete in a shooting contest. That's why, Hunter explained there were two shotguns, two assault rifles, and hundreds of rounds of ammunition stashed in his vehicle.

Yes, somebody had fired shots at the police. Hunter explained, but that was not his son. Instead he claimed the shooter was an unnamed passenger who just happened to blaze away at the cops. Hunter insisted his son had gotten out of the car before the chase began. But Indiana authorities scoffed at the Hunter story and brought the two to trial.

The Tippecanoe County jury found the senior Hunter guilty of attempted murder and several other felonies. But the younger Hunter was only convicted of receiving stolen property. Apparently the Hoosier jury believed the yarn that a John Doe was exchanging shots with police and not John Jr. It didn't matter much since the state case was only a "preliminary bout" to the federal bank robbery trial. And then the case took an unusual turn.

When the federal trial got underway in January, 1995, John Sr. turned sacrificial lamb. The elder Hunter made no bones about it. Yes, he testified, he had indeed robbed 19 mid-western banks during an 11 month period but denied that his son was involved in any of the heists. Apparently, if you bought Hunter's story, this is the way he obtained his "partners in crime." He would troll skid row areas and he would recruit people with serious financial problems. Hunter told the jury, "These were people who were willing to do anything to solve those (financial) problems." But Hunter could not name any of these alleged accomplices because as he put it, "We did not exchange personal information." The Hunter testimony brought a rebuttal from prosecutors Victoria Peters and Jerome Krulenitch They called the claim "laughable."

Actually the senior Hunter's attempt to fall on his sword made sense. He was facing an 80 year prison sentence in Indiana on the charge of attempted murder of two police officers. So he had nothing to lose in his federal trial gambit since he was already doomed to a life in prison.

As to the items found in the younger Hunter's home, defense attorneys indicated the incriminating evidence belonged to the father who had moved into his son's northwest suburban home in 1992. The items included a list of banks and locations, maps of cities where bank robberies had occurred, masks, and last but not least, clothing believed worn by the robbers.

The jury didn't swallow the senior Hunter's version of events and after some seven hours of deliberation it found the pair guilty of 16 bank jobs while armed with a gun. In April, 1995, Judge Marvin Aspen threw the book at the two men. Actually, the judge had no choice since mandatory federal sentencing laws required him to do so. The fact that the two men brandished handguns while holding up the banks gave the judge no option but to hand out draconian sentences

The defendants got public enemy Number One treatment at their sentencing. A force of U. S Marshals was in the courtroom and both men were handcuffed and shackled, even John Sr. who sat in a wheelchair because of a leg injury.

Before Judge Aspen handed down his sentence John Sr. addressed the court, admitting his guilt and denying again that his son had anything to do with the robberies. Said Hunter Sr., "An innocent boy is going to prison. I think that this is unfortunate."

The elder Hunter, who was then almost 57 years old, was handed a jail term of 377 years and seven months. The younger Hunter also got a life term, 316 years and seven months in a penitentiary. And prison it was for the Hunters. The father is whiling away his days at the Indiana State Prison in Michigan City on the attempted murder charges. His projected release date is June, 2033, when he will be 95 years old. If he is still in his golden years at that point Hunter will be transferred to a federal prison for another lengthy hitch. As to John Jr., the younger Hunter is doing time at the maximum security prison at Florence, Colorado, the toughest of the federal pens. His projected release date is March 4, 2271.

FBI"S David Childre, the agent assigned to the case, said the Hunter story was tragic. "They wasted their lives. They were both, educated, articulate, and capable."

Although the Hunters were the most prolific bank robbers in the Chicago area since World War II their exploits did not command the national attention of a contemporary. That would be Jeff Erickson, the Bearded Bandit. Erickson, who wore a fake beard on the job, was charged with eight bank robberies although his lawyer said the true count was closer to 20. The scores between January of 1990 and November of 1991 netted Erickson around $180,000.

There was nothing in Erickson's background to indicate that he would end up leading a life of crime. In fact he spent 13 months as a police trainee in a Chicago suburb. But a life in law enforcement was not in the cards for Erickson. Friends said that Erickson was a superb marksman, certainly an asset for a police officer. However, others said he was too nice a guy to be a cop. Apparently Erickson felt guilty in stopping people and writing them a ticket. That description flies in the face of the Erickson who threatened to shoot tellers if they failed to obey his commands to hand over the money. Erickson, with his brief law enforcement career over, switched horses and became a used book store owner in the Chicago suburb of Roselle.

Erickson had one hobby, a motorbike, and he shared that passion with a woman, Jill Cohen, who was soon to become his wife. Jill, authorities said, was something of a free spirit but with a bi-polar disorder leaving her with violent mood swings She was no stranger to firearms. Co-workers said she often carried a gun when she came to work. Erickson once told investigators after his capture that he had trained his wife in the use of firearms There was no question investigators said that Jill was a willing participant with her husband in Jeff's bank robbery schemes.

It is not known how many robberies the two pulled together. But there was at least one instance where the duo became a modern day Bonnie and Clyde. That was December 16, 1991, only this time Bonnie died and Clyde was captured.

The two were using separate getaway cars in a northwest suburban bank heist. Jeff was in a stolen Mazda and Jill in a Ford Econoline.

However a contingent of law enforcement personnel had staked out the area. FBI agents and suburban police surrounded Erickson's car in a Schaumburg parking lot and the Bearded Bandit surrendered without offering any resistance. This was in sharp contrast to an earlier incident when Erickson wounded a police officer who was trying to apprehend him. With Jill though, it turned out to be a different story.

Jill tried to flee and led police on a wild chase through the northwest suburbs with speeds reaching close to 100 miles per hour. She exchanged shots with her pursuers before her van struck a wall in Hanover Park. It was there, lawmen said, that Jill committed suicide by shooting herself in the face with a .45. Erickson never believed the story and thought it was the police who had killed his wife. His obsession with his wife's death might have influenced his later actions which led to a bloody shootout in the federal building.

With Erickson under lock and key at the Metropolitan Correctional Center and Jill dead, authorities began piecing together details about the man know as the Bearded Bandit. When former FBI agent David Childre and his colleagues visited the Erickson's suburban home they got an eyeful. They found a cache of weapons, some 38 shotguns, rifles, and handguns, as well as a couple dozen ammunition boxes. Also on hand were a number of items that the well-heeled criminal should have. They included gas masks, smoke grenades, knives, fake mustaches, two fake beards, makeup remover, sun glasses, a police scanner, and bullet proof vests. Agent Childre told me that he is convinced that if the Ericksons would have been home at the time of the raid there would have been trouble. Said Childre, "I'm glad we didn't confront them at the home. There would have been a shootout."

The arsenal stunned residents who had known Erickson through his Roselle bookstore, Best Used Books, an establishment where you had to pay cash if you wanted to buy a book. I recall interviewing a man who operated a coin shop in the same shopping mall. He just couldn't believe that the Erickson he knew robbed banks. Other area merchants voiced the same surprise, except one. This merchant smelled a rat because she couldn't understand how Erickson could pay the rent in the mall when his store did such little business.

Erickson went on trial in the summer of 1992. The proceedings went according to Hoyle, and there seemed little doubt that Erickson would be convicted. And then something happened that gave Jeff Erickson his 15 minutes of fame.

It all happened on the late afternoon of July 20, 1992, with the trial over for the day and the husky defendant being led from the basement of the Dirksen Federal Building to the Metropolitan Correctional Center in downtown Chicago, where he was being held. Erickson never made it to the MCC.

In a desperate bid for freedom the 33 year old Erickson unlocked his handcuffs with a key, disarmed a federal guard, fatally shot a U.S. Deputy Marshall, and killed a court security officer. Although mortally wounded, the court security officer, Harry Belluomini, fired four shots from his gun striking Erickson in the back. Wounded, the bank robber, armed with a 357 magnum staggered up the ramp of the courthouse. Erickson had grabbed the gun from one of the security guards after he had freed himself. But Erickson never made it to the street. Belluomini's shot had done the trick. Collapsing to the ground Erickson, realizing his wound was fatal, grabbed his gun and shot himself in the head.

The incident in the basement of the federal building was the lead story on TV newscasts that night and made headlines in the morning newspapers the following day. The escape raised questions as to how a dangerous criminal was handled by the marshal's service. The $64,000—question was how did Erickson get the keys to unlock his handcuffs? Authorities put on a full court press in an effort to determine who had supplied the key to Erickson.

Erickson's mother and brother had visited the MCC two days before the escape attempt, but they denied sneaking a

Jeff Erickson. Killed in Dirksen Building shootout. FBI photo.

handcuff key to the prisoner. Jail guards were also questioned but they could shed no light on the matter. An inmate at the MCC said Erickson had told him that he had a handcuff key, and the inmate claimed when he doubted Erickson's story the Bearded Bandit opened his mouth and displayed what appeared to be some sort of metal object.

The mystery of the escape was finally solved some ten years after the bloody Dirksen shootout. Robert Burke, a con man, was convicted on perjury charges when he denied in a grand jury appearance that he had slipped the handcuff key to Erickson. Prosecutors put several inmates on the stand who were incarcerated at the MCC in 1992. They told the jury that Burke had told them that he was the one who had supplied the handcuff key to Erickson. Government lawyers indicated that Erickson was to pay Burke $2,000 for the key. Whether Burke received the payoff is not known. Judge Rebecca Pallmeyer sentenced the 52 year old Burke to a 20 year prison term. That's very close to a lifetime sentence for a middle aged man.

The saga of Jeffrey Erickson and his wife Jill was just too good for Hollywood to ignore. Three years after Erickson died on the Dirksen Federal Building ramp, a movie about the bank robbing duo was filmed in Chicago. It starred Luke Perry and Ashley Judd in the roles of Jeff and Jill. But the bank robbing pair were given phony names and so too were the suburbs of Schaumburg and Roselle. The producers did take some dramatic license but the film was a takeoff on the Erickson saga, complete with the shoot out in the basement of the federal building. The film never made it to the silver screen and ended up as a made for TV movie.

Although the Flesh Masked Bandits and the Bearded Bandit garnered the headlines and raked in the most cash, other robbers also used disguises or unusual M.O.'s when carrying out their heists. The FBI office in Chicago was quick to give these felons different monikers.

For example, there was the Dapper Dan Bandit, so named because of his dapper attire. He would stroll into banks wearing a camel haired coat and a black fedora. His score amounted to $105,000 before he was caught and sentenced to six and a half years.

Then there was the Bomber Bandit who brandished a fake bomb when carrying out his bank robbing tasks. He would take a device out his brief case which he said was a bomb. The so-called bomb was just a black box with a blinking red light. He demanded money and claimed he could detonate the bomb by remote control.

Let's not forget the Apologetic Bandit. That's because he usually apologized to the bank teller. He would say after he pulled his job, "Have a nice day." Then the Apologetic Ban-

The Leaping Bandit. Bank photo.

dit would walk out of the bank with what he thought was a task well done.

How about the Zombie Bandit who because of his stiff gait, bulging eyes, monotone voice, and pockmarked face got the Zombie nickname. It turned out the Zombie bandit was a Michigan educator with a Ph.D. He hit eight banks in a four state area before he was caught.

Then there was the Lunch Bag Bandit. He didn't necessarily strike at lunch time, but he would put his stolen bank cash into green paper bags. The Lunch Bag Bandit got four years in the "hoosegow" for knocking off five banks in a one month stretch.

Others who did "monkey business" in lending institutions included, The Beer Barrel Bandit. You got it, he had a paunch. And he was also no spring chicken. He was 70 years old when he plied his trade. The Clearasil Bandit on the other hand had an acne problem. The Gentlemen Bandit didn't act like a rogue. The Clown Bandit, wore clown garb. The Leaping Bandit would vault over the counter, pistol in hand, to get his loot. The Hot Pink Bandit would wear nothing but pink. The Lunchtime Bandit preferred his heists at mid-day. The Santa Bandit struck at Christmas time wearing a Santa Claus suit. The Ray Ban Style Bandit had aviation style glasses on his "schoznola." An alcoholic, he pulled six jobs before he was caught.

There have been many more. Who could forget the Plain Jane Bandit, named because she had average looks and drew no attention to herself. She wore no disguises and would stand in line with the other customers. When it was her turn she would slip a note to bank employee demanding money. She implied the teller would be shot if the bank employee would not cooperate.

Even senior citizens got into the act. There was the Grandpa Bandit, a 77 year old World War II vet. He got three years in prison for robbing three north suburban banks. The Grandpa Bandit told the sentencing judge he needed the money to take out a 78 year old girlfriend. Showing remorse the elderly bandit laid his cards on the table by saying, "I can't believe I could do something so stupid."

Not all these modern day Dillingers are playing with a full deck. Some readers may remember Woody Allen playing the world's most inept bank robber in the 1969 film, *Take The Money and Run.* But a botched 1999 job at a bank in Chicago takes the cake. The robber handed a note to a teller claiming he had two bombs. He demanded $45,000. A bank officer suggested the robber relax for a few minutes until an executive okayed the transaction. The robber complies with the request. He sat down with the bank officer and batted the breeze while waiting for his money. By this time the police arrived and the hapless bank robber was taken into custody.

But not all bank robberies end so peacefully. Sometimes gun play is involved and sometimes individuals get hurt and even killed. Not that this is the norm. It doesn't happen often but it happens too much as far as authorities are concerned.

In the small northwest Indiana town of Pines, a teller was shot and killed at a branch of the First State Bank of Porter. Another teller was wounded, as well as a security guard in the 2002 incident. The bandits got nothing and all four were later arrested.

In February, 2003, a 70 year old bank vice-president was shot in the leg while opening a southwest side bank. There have been other incidents too, but in most cases no bank employees or customers were harmed.

The same year that the bank executive was shot in the leg there was a "dog day afternoon" in south suburban Plainfield. The bandit held four hostages captive for four hours. He released each hostage at intervals before walking out of the bank, raising his hands and surrendering. Nobody got hurt but there were some anxious moments.

Sometimes when there is gun play, the bad guys bite the dust. In 1996 an off duty cop killed a robber after the bandit had pulled a score at a small branch bank in the Edgewater neighborhood of Chicago. The shooting occurred outside the bank. Then in 1999 a man walked into the LaSalle National Bank, flashed a handgun, and escaped with an unknown amount of cash. But ten blocks from the holdup scene a plainclothes policeman shot and killed the man.

There is a discouraging note of late. The FBI says the heists are getting more violent. The Bureau says the number of what it described as takeover robberies has increased in the last few years. A takeover robbery occurs when the bandit or bandits display a weapon, then demand everyone hit the floor, or if not that the robbers will herd employees and customers into the vault or another area of the facility while they clean out the drawers. According to the FBI about 20 percent of the bank robberies in the Chicago area in 2005 could be described as some kind of takeover job.

In 2005 a record 236 bank robberies occurred in the Chicago area. That compares to 161 in the same period in 2004. The 236 figure was compiled from a six county area— Cook, DuPage, Lake, Will, Kendall, and Kane Counties. The number of people injured in the year was less than 15 and most of those were minor injuries.

Why are more banks being held up? Observers give different reasons in trying to pin down the hike in robberies.

First of all there are more banks. Personally I feel the growing number of branch banks is the number one reason. Many of these facilities are located in shopping malls, supermarkets, or in combination drug and convenience stores. They provide the robber with easy automotive access to get in and out in a hurry. The small banks don't have the security personnel that larger and older downtown banks have. And the branch banks often have longer hours giving the robber more opportunity to ply his or her trade. As Chicago FBI agent Ross Rice puts it, "The more banks you have and the longer they're open, the more possibility that one is going to be robbed."

Economic conditions are also a factor. When times are not the best, people who need a quick buck find it awfully tempting to go where the money is: a bank.

Officials with the American Bankers Association estimate close to 50 percent of bank robbers are drug users. A case in point was the tragic story of a 64 year old Lewiston, Illinois, man who became hooked on crack cocaine. A village trustee and a volunteer firefighter, he staged a series of bank robberies to finance his habit. He was sentenced in December, 2005, to a 40 year prison term, a life term for a man his age. Ironically, he was turned in by his three sons, one a police officer.

The police officer recognized "dear old Dad" on a bank's surveillance tape.

Robert Grant, the FBI Agent In Charge of the Chicago office, estimates that the average haul in a bank job is about $2,000. Considering that a robber can get up to ten years in prison if he or she brandishes a weapon or threatens to use a weapon, a bank job doesn't seem worth the risk. And when you consider that most bank robbers are eventually caught, it doesn't seem the right career path to choose if you want to enter a life of crime.

There are steps that banks can take to increase security and help deter robberies. But smaller banks often don't want to spend money to hire more security guards (if they even have one) or install high tech cameras or other detection gear. They figure the average robbers take only about $2,000 and with much of the stolen cash insured it's just not worth it.

There is another factor too. Too much security, such as bullet resistant partitions, more armed security guards, and metal detectors could scare off some customers. An "O.K. Corral" situation with security guards shooting it out with robber could be counter productive. Some customers could get hurt and the banks could be liable.

But even if banks were to make their facilities much more secure to discourage robbers, it probably wouldn't stop desperate criminals because, after all, the banks are where the money is.

A postscript: Chicago area bank robberies continued to climb in 2006 setting another record. A total of 284 banks were held up in that year. That's over forty more bank jobs compared to the previous year.

12

ON THE LAM

It was described by the U.S. Attorney for the Northern District of Illinois, William Bauer, as the largest bank fraud and embezzlement in the nation's history. That was in 1971 when the government contended that four men had embezzled the princely sum of $6,779,450 from the Cosmopolitan Bank of Chicago.

Three of the defendants had been officials of the Steinberg-Baum Company, a Chicago area discount store. One of those indicted was Louis Steinberg, then a 48 year old resident of Highland Park, who was the firm's vice-president.

The May, 1971 indictment received a great deal of play in the Chicago media. But when it came time to surrender, one of the men was conspicuous by his absence. That was Steinberg, who didn't stroll into the Dirksen Federal Building to face the music. No, Steinberg was a long way from Chicago when the indictment came down.

In fact Steinberg wasn't even in the States; he had fled to Rhodesia which had no extradition treaty with the U.S.

Actually Steinberg, apparently fearing that bad news was imminent, had left for Europe about April 15th, two weeks before the indictment was returned. From Europe he flew to Salisbury, then the capital of Rhodesia. Government officials said he was living "high off the hog" in Africa where he operated a lucrative auction house and married a beautiful Eurasian woman.

While Steinberg sojourned in Rhodesia, his fellow defendants in the scheme all were convicted, including Frank Baum, the President of the eleven store discount chain. Baum was sentenced to three years in prison followed by two years of probation.

Then some seven years after he was indicted Steinberg voluntarily returned to Chicago to face charges in connection with the embezzlement scheme. Many observers were puzzled by his decision. Why would Steinberg leave a sanctuary where he was immune from the long arm of the law, where he was a successful businessman, and where he had a small child?

Louis Steinberg arrives back in Chicago from Rhodesia. WBBM-TV photo.

When Steinberg returned to Chicago in July of 1978 he was surrounded by U.S. Marshals at O'Hare Field and would not talk to reporters. But that all changed several weeks later when Steinberg was released from the Metropolitan Correctional Center after posting $400,000 bond. In those days cameras were permitted on the 20th floor of the Dirksen Federal Building when criminal defendants posted bond before walking out of the courthouse. It was there that Steinberg seemed eager to talk to the media.

He explained why he had come back to Chicago saying, "I love my country and I had to come back because I'm getting on in age" (he was 55 at the time). Steinberg added that he wanted to settle down and start all over again, pointing out that he had been born and raised in Chicago. He predicted that day he would be vindicated on the embezzlement and tax charge.

Despite Steinberg's professed love of country cynics took a different view as to why he ended his self-imposed exile. When Steinberg fled to Africa, Rhodesia was an independent nation with a very small white minority in control. It had been a British possession and, under a 1961 constitution, voting was restricted to keep whites in power. For example, white farmers made up less than one percent of the population, yet held seventy percent of the arable land. But that all changed and guerrilla warfare became a fact of life. Whites began leaving the country. Violence became commonplace in Rhodesia and it was a very tense situation. Justice Department officials felt the changing political climate was the real reason that Steinberg came back. Rhodesia in 1980 became Zimbabwe and shrugged off British control. It is an independent nation, although plagued by a ruthless dictatorial regime.

Steinberg hired a prominent defense attorney, George Cotsirilos, and moved to South Carolina to begin a new life. When he returned for the trial he had hired a different lawyer to represent him. Steinberg proclaimed his innocence, claiming that he didn't steal any money, arguing that he had always intended to pay it back. However, after deliberating seven hours the jury felt that didn't hold water. It found Steinberg guilty on most counts in the six count indictment.

On February 23, 1979 Steinberg was sentenced to ten years in a federal prison despite a plea for mercy from the defendant. Federal Judge George Leighton turned a deaf ear to Steinberg's exhortations, summing it up this way, "He embezzled, he purloined, he stole."

When firefighters arrived at the 22 room Barrington Hills mansion of Marvin and Kaye Lichtman on January 23, 1996, the entire home was already engulfed in flames. The firefighters did not know that the 78 year old Lichtman and his 75 year old wife, a wealthy retired couple, were already dead. What appeared at first to be a fire tragedy turned out to be a homicide. The elderly couple had not perished because of fire or smoke inhalation. They had been shot to death. The remains of their beloved dog, Mr. Duke, were also found.

Authorities theorized that the killer first murdered Kaye, who was home alone at the time. Husband Marvin had been out of town and apparently the killer was waiting for him to arrive. Lieutenant Lou Tessmann of the Lake County Major Crimes Task Force explained, "When he came home a limousine dropped him off. His body was recovered inside the front door so our assumption was, when he got home, he was shot immediately, inside the front door of the residence." Police believed the Lichtman's 14,000 square foot mansion was set on fire to cover up the double homicide.

It didn't take Lake County authorities long before zeroing in on their prime suspect. He was Peter Hommerson, who grew up in Hungary before coming to the states in 1979. Hommerson was sort of a handy man, had done work for the Lichtmans, was very familiar with the property and most importantly, was seen by witnesses in and around the house on the day of the fire.

Manetta Quillinan, the Lichtman niece, told Channel Two News that Hommerson had known her aunt and uncle for sev-

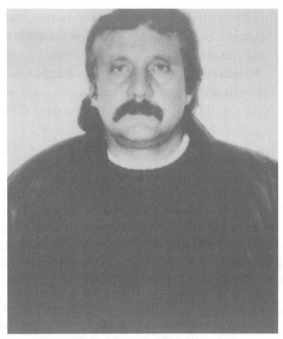

Peter Hommerson—apprehended in Mexico.

eral years. She said she believed they trusted him. According to Manetta, "He had done some glass work, had installed some bar stools, and was beginning to work on a glass sketching of Marin, Kaye, and the dog, Mr. Duke." And the Lichtman niece added, "Kaye had a habit of keeping a lot of cash around." The couple also had an extensive art collection in the home, in addition to a number of valuable vases.

It seemed the more authorities knew about Hommerson, the more they felt he was their man. He had financial problems, which gave him a motive and had the opportunity to do the crime. In addition to that, he failed a lie detector test. Then when investigators went to his Algonquin home they found pieces of evidence, including a vase left in his van. However, there was one fly in the ointment—his wife, Ros Hommerson, gave him an alibi.

The alibi, though later fell apart. According to Lt. Tessmann, Ros Hommerson later recanted and admitted that her husband had called her and asked her to make up an alibi for his whereabouts. What prompted Ros Hommerson to recant her story is anybody's guess. The two had gone to Hannibal, Missouri, after the slayings and then headed for Laredo, Texas. It was there Hommerson, who did not have a passport, said goodbye to his wife, crossed over the border to Nuevo Laredo, and disappeared.

By then, Hommerson had been charged with first degree murder and a $1,000,000 reward had been issued for his arrest and conviction. Despite an international manhunt Hommerson was not apprehended. Some lawmen felt Hommerson could have gone back to his native Hungary. He was supposedly fluent in a number of languages, meaning he could be anywhere on the European continent. Or then again maybe he was hiding out in Mexico where he was last seen.

For over nine years Hommerson continued to elude authorities. He was the subject on eight episodes of the television program *America's Most Wanted.* But nothing happened until April, 2003, when two vacationing American couples saw his face on the show. They had been in the Mexican resort community of Ixtapa and had stopped at a restaurant called LaYarda. They remembered the genial proprietor, who they thought was a dead ringer for the man on *America's Most Wanted.*

The FBI was notified and Mexican authorities were contacted. When the "Federales" went to the restaurant, Hommerson showed them a phony ID in the name of one Pedro Ruiz Herman Vargas. Hommerson or Vargas as he called himself had married a Mexican woman and together they ran the bar and restaurant. But Mexican authorities weren't fooled by the phony ID and soon Hommerson threw in the towel and allegedly said, "It's me, you've got me."

The 60 year old Hommerson was deported and put on a plane to Houston and waived extradition to Lake County where he faced murder charges. In some ways lawmen said it appeared Hommeson was relieved that it was all over. Perhaps he got tired of looking over his shoulder.

Then there was the case of the man who walked away from a minimum security prison in Massachusetts and spent at least 18 years on the lam in Chicago. He was Norman Porter, a twice convicted killer, who was known in Chicago as J.J. Jameson. In the media he was given the sobriquet of the "Killer Poet."

Porter soon became something of a character after he arrived in Chicago on a Greyhound bus. When he walked out of the bus station in the loop he had close to $3,000 on him, money he had earned doing landscaping work while he was incarcerated. It's unclear why Porter selected Chicago as his new home, although friends said he was enchanted with Chicago author Nelson Algren's *City On The Make.* Apparently Porter was eager to visit some of the locations mentioned in the Algren classic.

After making a deal with a home owner for free rent in exchange for being the building's handyman, Porter was set. He parlayed his skill as a handyman to receive free lodging in apartments, three flats, and a home in suburban Maywood. He even worked on Mayor Harold Washington's 1987 campaign which revealed he was in Chicago for at least 18 years prior to his arrest in March, 2005.

Porter soon became a favorite of the city's bohemian element. He was a regular on the poetry scene and often showed up at sessions of the College of Complexes, a raucous political discussion group that traced its roots to Chicago's famed Bughouse Square. He was an anti-war activist, an interesting speaker and conversationalist, albeit a cantankerous one.

He supported himself doing odd jobs and maintenance work but apparently never told anyone about his violent past.

Porter's life as J.J. Jameson, the well-liked poet, came to a sudden end in March, 2005, when he was arrested at a far west side church. It seemed that Massachusetts State Police had gotten wind that Porter could be living in Chicago. After the FBI matched Porter's fingerprints to an arrest of Jameson in Chicago in the early 1990s, the Bay State fugitive squad moved quickly. After all they had been looking for Porter since he dropped off the face of the earth in 1985. So the "Killer Poet," as he was called was returned to Massachusetts and a date with a judge.

The 65 year old Porter felt he should get a break, pointing out that he had helped the homeless, did other charitable things, and was not involved in any serious trouble while living in the Midwest metropolis. He claimed he had straightened himself out.

Actually Porter didn't fare too badly in court. In October, 2005, he pleaded guilty to the escape charge and was sentenced to three more years in prison. The three year hitch would not begin until Porter completed a life sentence for the 1960 murder of a clothing store clerk. His second murder conviction had been commuted years earlier by then Governor Michael Dukakis. After the sentencing on the escape charge his lawyer told reporters that his client would be eligible for parole after about five years. So the 18 year adventure as a fugitive only cost Porter about three years.

Who knows, the "Killer Poet" could someday come back to Chicago to visit his old haunts that he liked so well.

Outfit guys are notorious for taking off like a "bat out of Hell" when an indictment is near. South suburban rackets' boss Albert Tocco fled to Greece when the Feds were closing in. He was later expelled from Greece and turned up in Rome where he was provided with an FBI escort back to Chicago.

Joey "The Clown" Lombardo evaded the long arm of the law for nine months before he was arrested in suburban Elmwood Park. His April, 2005, indictment touched off an international manhunt with some "insiders" saying he had gone to the Bahamas or the Caribbean island of Curacao.

We received a letter at WBBM-TV shortly after Lombardo disappeared saying Lombardo was either in Chicago or just over the state line in Wisconsin. Turned out, he had been in Elmwood Park. At least that was where the FBI found him.

Another mobster who vanished after being indicted in the April, 2005, Family Secrets case was Frank "The German" Schweihs. Seers said that Schweihs, like Lombardo, was sunning himself in the Caribbean. But Schweihs was not in the tropics. He was apprehended, after eight months on the run, in Berea, Kentucky, right in the heart of the Bible Belt.

Berea Police Lieutenant Ken Clark told reporters after Schweihs' arrest, "This is probably the biggest fish we ever got in our little pond."

Sometimes a criminal already in custody goes on the lam by escaping from the "Big House." I got a call one early morning from a federal source in May, 1985, that two dangerous "cons" had escaped from the Metropolitan Correctional Center (MCC), the federal lockup in downtown Chicago. The two escapees were not white collar criminals waiting to be transferred to some "club fed' in Florida or California. They were men who had long records and were not to be taken lightly by law enforcement personnel.

One of them was Bernard Welch, who achieved notoriety in 1980 for the fatal shooting of Dr. Michael Halberstam, the brother of famed journalist, David Halberstam. Dr. Halberstam was slain outside his Washington D.C. home after he surprised Welch during a burglary at the doctor's house.

Welch, of Great Falls, Virginia, was a master criminal, who was described by one police officer as "One of the most prolific burglars in the recent annals of American crime."

Welch drove to his jobs in a Mercedes-Benz and was not your typical breaking and entering artist. He was known as the multi-millionaire burglar because he only broke into homes of the well-to-do.

But lawmen figured he would no longer be a thorn in their side after he was sentenced to 143 years for the murder of Dr. Halberstam. Before coming to the MCC, Welch had done time in maximum security prisons in Marion, Illinois, and Atlanta, Georgia. Jail officials knew his penchant for "going over the wall." In 1974 he had escaped from a medium security prison near Dannemora, New York.

His partner in the Chicago escape was Hugh Colomb of Rutland, Vermont, not exactly a Mr. Rogers either. Colomb, who had a prior escape record and was doing a 48 year stretch for robbery, was also convicted of killing another prison inmate and assaulting a federal officer.

With track records like that the reader may wonder why the two men were housed at a holding center like the MCC rather than a tough prison like Marion, then considered the "new Alcatraz." At a news conference, the morning after the escape the warden, O.C. Jenkins, said the two men had been supplying information about escape plans and potential attacks on guards at other institutions, and that's why the two had been brought to the MCC.

But authorities later conceded that Welch and Colomb had conned prison officials into believing that they were cooperating in a federal investigation. Whether their information was the "Real McCoy" or bogus, they got what they wanted, a transfer to the MCC where they had a better chance to escape.

And escape they did in the middle of the night during a driving rainstorm. Because of their alleged cooperation the two inmates were wearing their own clothes. At the time of the escape, MCC policy allowed personnel in protective custody to wear civilian garb. However, the question remained, even in their own clothes, how did the two men escape from the sixth floor?

Investigators said Welch and Colomb had punched a hole in the seven inch cinder block wall of the facility with a barbell. They also used a hacksaw blade to enhance the hole that they had made. Then the two men took a 75 foot long cord on a floor buffer, which they used as a rope to descend down to the ground level below. The cord was tied to the floor buffer which was adjacent to the wall and held the cord as they slid to freedom.

The escape touched off a massive search for the two desperados, whose escape had embarrassed prison officials. Two other inmates and a woman were charged with aiding the escape by smuggling a hacksaw blade to Colomb. With the exception of a 1975 escape from the supposedly escape proof Marion prison in 1975, the Welch and Colomb break out was the most publicized jail break in Illinois since Roger "The Terrible" Touhy and Basil "The Owl" Banghart went over the wall at Stateville in the early 1940s.

Although Welch had been dubbed the "Society Burglar" because his victims were in the big bucks, he was considered the more dangerous of the two. Welch's former lawyer Sol Rosen gave him quite a buildup calling him, "The most dangerous criminal in American history."

Welch's stay in freedom was short lived. He was apprehended about three months after his escape. The end came in Greensberg, Pennsylvania, a community of some 20,000 residents. Welch had been busy during those three months. Police believe he was responsible for a one man crime spree in the affluent Milwaukee suburb of Shorewood. He was captured out east when police on routine patrol spotted his stolen BMW outside his Greensberg apartment building. That BMW had been reported stolen by a Shorewood, Wisconsin, resident on May 26, 1985, eleven days after the men had broken out of the MCC.

It was by chance that the Greensberg police came across Welch. They were answering a complaint about an illegally parked car which turned out to be stolen. When the officers went to the apartment building to determine who had been driving the BMW, a woman on the third floor said the vehicle belonged to her boy friend, one Robert Wilson. The two patrolmen awoke the man who said he was Robert Wilson. The cops then took him to the station house where a fingerprint check revealed he was the master criminal Robert Welch. A search by police of Welch's car and the apartment found what was described as a large quantity of stolen property.

Officials, not wanting to see Welch pull a "Houdini stunt," again shipped him to the federal prison at Marion, Illinois, then the Bureau of Prisons' Super Max. According to the Bureau of Prisons, Welch died in jail in 1998. He was 58 years old.

Colomb didn't fare much better. The 31 year old Colomb was arrested in Canton, Mississippi, moments after he had pulled off a bank job with a sawed-off shotgun. Colomb was tightlipped as to where he had been during the five months that he had been a federal fugitive. Like his partner, Welch, Colomb was sent to a maximum security institution where hard men do hard time.

He wasn't the biggest fish in the fugitive pond but Nick Montos, a burglar with syndicate ties, was on the lam for nine years before he was subdued, not by police but by a 73 year old grandmother.

Montos failed to appear in Lake County, Indiana, court in 1986 for an arraignment on charges that he and three other men hauled away $100,000 worth of merchandise from the Woodman Jewelry Store in Hammond. Montos, who was 69 when he vanished, had a rap sheet dating back to the early

1930s. He was only a teenager then but apparently had plenty of street smarts.

Lake County Prosecutor John Burke told me in 1989, "I've been involved in the prosecution business for 16 years and I've never seen an individual who has as extensive a criminal record as Nick Montos. He was born in 1916 and his first conviction, that I'm aware of was in 1930, so he was about 14 years old when he was first convicted. He's been in and out of prison virtually all of his life."

Don't get the idea that "Little Nicky," he was only five feet four inches tall, was strictly a breaking and entering guy. Uncle Sam was suspicious that Montos was involved in heavy stuff. He was a suspect in the 1975 murder of August Maniaci and spent 18 months in the Waukesha County Jail when he refused to testify before a grand jury investigating the Maniaci homicide. However, Montos was never charged with any involvement in the murder.

Nick Montos met his match with an old woman.

Montos became a fugitive from justice when he apparently felt that Hammond authorities had the goods on him. He was convicted in absentia on the jewelry store job and also of trying to blow up a pursuing squad car. Montos was no stranger to being on the lam. He once escaped from a chain gang in Alabama where he was doing time. And he knew what hard time was. He had been incarcerated at Alcatraz, the "Rock," so he had had his fill of prison life.

Montos took off for Greece and reportedly was living very comfortably in a suburb of Athens. Police told Channel Two News that because Montos' parents had been born in Greece and that he held dual citizenship, he could not be extradited. But Montos became homesick for the States. He sent an audio tape to his wife in suburban River Forest apologizing that he had fled, explaining, "I don't want to die in prison."

Then in 1995, Montos left Greece, entering the U.S. in Houston under the name of Oliver Keller. From Texas he headed east, winding up in Boston where his criminal career came to an abrupt halt. Nick was not one to pass up what he thought would be an easy score, and he felt an antique store run by a 73 year old woman in the Boston suburb of Brookline would fill the bill.

So, Montos came to the shop of Sonia Paine, a grandmother, and waved his piece at her, telling Sonia to shut up and keep quiet. When Mrs. Paine, who was hard of hearing, kept yapping away, Montos taped her wrists together and then began rifling jewelry cases.

But Mrs. Paine, a Polish refugee, wiggled out of the tape while Montos looked for swag. She grabbed a Louisville Slugger and hit Montos on the head as he was examining her safe. Stunned, Montos was knocked off his feet but then got up and hit Mrs. Paine with his gun. Unknown to Nick the grandmother had been able to activate a silent police alarm. The diminutive Montos fled to a back room in the store and when a police officer arrived, Nick aimed his handgun at the cop. Enter Grandmother Paine again. She hit Montos in the back of the neck with the bat and the policeman took Montos into custody.

The would-be robber, sporting a king sized headache, ended up in the hospital where he was swathed in bandages. His opponent also was taken to the hospital where she was stitched up. Montos faced a variety of charges for his ill fated robbery attempt including armed robbery and assault and battery with intent to kill.

For Nick Montos, who had mixed it up with the best of them, it was ironic that he was able to elude John Law for 18 years, only to be taken down by a grandmother.

Don't get the idea that all fugitives are caught. They aren't. Some are never apprehended and often end up in foreign lands. A case in point was Chicagoan Nick Stevens, indicted in Operation Safebet. Nick high tailed it to Greece where he apparently found a home.

Then there is the case of "Terrible" Tommy O'Connor. Tommy was being held in the old Cook County Jail awaiting to be hanged for murdering a police officer. But O'Connor

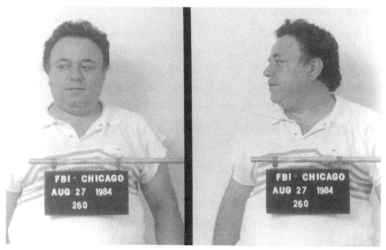

Nick Stevens
The government believes he fled to Greece.

busted out of the jail in 1921, cheating the hangman's noose. "Terrible Tommy" hasn't been seen since. For years jail officials kept the gallows on which he was to be hanged. But, as time passed, officials realized that Tommy must have gone to his eternal reward, so the gallows were dismantled.

13

THE STONES

There are some police officers who say the Blackstone Rangers were at one time one of the most powerful street gangs in the country. In its heyday, from the late 1960s to the late 1980s, the group changed its identity several times. The Rangers became the Black P. Stone Nation and later evolved into an organization calling itself the El Rukns. Some in the community always referred to the gang as the Stones.

The Stones' turf was originally in the Woodlawn area on the south side of Chicago. The Rangers got their start in 1964 around 64th street and Blackstone Avenue, hence the Blackstone moniker. Violence and fear were their trademark and their income was derived from narcotics, prostitution, and the old protection racket. For a time the Rangers took over the old Southmoor Hotel which, in it's prime, was the scene of many parties when the University of Chicago Maroons were a force to be reckoned with on the gridiron. It was easy to spot a Ranger—members could be identified by the red tams that adorned their heads.

During the riots that followed the assassination of Dr. Martin Luther King in 1968, the south side of Chicago was relatively quiet while the west side erupted into violence, burning and looting. There are those who contend that city officials made a deal with the Blackstone Rangers to keep a lid on the south side. Such a deal has never been substantiated. The city has denied it but for whatever reason the Rangers did not take part in the Chicago disturbances.

It was at that time the Rangers were adopted by the radical left who apparently felt that the gang could be a force for good. The Rangers' leaders, including Jeff Fort, were entertained at cocktail parties hosted by wealthy Chicagoans. The Stones also got the attention of others who could be described as "do gooders." Denver millionaire Charles Kettering II gave thousands of dollars for Rangers' bond money and legal funds. Uncle Sam also kicked in. The Federal Government handed the Rangers almost a million dollars for a job training grant. Its purpose was to train south side youngsters in vocational skills. Fort, the Rangers strongman, was hired as a youth center director.

Jeff Fort—Police mug shot of Chicago's top street gang boss.

Fort was even invited to attend President Richard Nixon's first inauguration in 1969. Fort declined the honor but sent two of his subordinates to represent the Rangers at the festivities.

But Fort and company soon ran afoul of Uncle Sam. That hefty government grant was too tempting to the Stones. The gang, according to the Justice Department, used the money to finance its own operations, not to train inner city youths. In other words, some of the money went to buy guns and drugs.

That aroused the ire of Senator John McClellan, the veteran Democrat from Arkansas, who held hearings to investigate what happened. McClellan had seen crime syndicate chieftains like Tony Accardo appear before his committee, but Fort was something else. The 21 year old Fort showed up wearing wrap around sun glasses, a tall Afro, and a jump suit. He answered a few questions, then gave a Black Power salute and walked out. He was held in contempt of Congress. He ended up doing time in a federal prison.

Fort spent two years in the federal penitentiary in Leavenworth, Kansas.

However, despite his incarceration, Fort's hold over his gang never waned. In fact it was there that he crowned himself, "Prince Malik" and changed the name of the gang from the Blackstone P. Nation to the El Rukns.

Jeff Fort was not a native Chicagoan. He was born in Aberdeen, Mississippi, in 1947 and like many African-American families of that period, Fort's parents, along with Jeff and his siblings, moved north to Chicago in search of a better job and greater opportunities. Jeff's father got work in a steel mill and the family settled in on the south side. Fort allegedly attended Hyde Park High School but dropped out before he got a diploma. Other reports said he never got beyond the fourth grade. One thing is certain, the future El Rukn leader had things on his mind other than reading, writing, and arithmetic. Fort was not a big guy but he bulked up in prison, apparently from pumping iron.

Despite his youth Fort, who had the nickname Angel, had plenty of street smarts and it wasn't long before he teamed up with Eugene "Bull" Hairston, one of the original bosses of the Blackstone Rangers. Before long a number of rival street gangs got the message and pooled their talents with the Rangers to become the Blackstone P. Nation.

Hairston, a tough customer, although not necessarily the brightest, was considered the top "Stone." Hairston's reign though was short lived because in June, 1966, "Bull" was sentenced to prison. Fort became "numero uno," a position he continues to hold today. When Hairston was released from prison, two years later, he was no longer a factor in the gang's hierarchy. Hairston survived one assassination attempt and ended up a small time drug dealer. Murdered in a Chicago housing project in 1988, his death received little fanfare.

Jeff Fort leaves Criminal Courts building, surrounded by henchmen.

Fort's other rivals or would be heirs also met untimely demises. With Jeff periodically doing time in the Big House for a number of indiscretions it was only natural that some of his colleagues would covet his throne.

The only serious contender was Henry "Mickey Cobb" Cogwell. Cogwell was a member of the group's Main 21, or what I call the gangs' Politburo. Cogwell was a bright young man who had attended the 1969 Nixon inauguration in place of Fort. He represented the gang in dealings with the media and came across quite well. Reportedly Cogwell was the Stones' contact with the Chicago Mob when such things as disputes over territory would erupt. But "Mickey Cobb" signed his own death warrant, according to some investigators, when he objected to Fort's plan of turning the Blackstone P. Nation into the El Rukns. In1977 Cogwell was fatally shot in the chest and head only a short distance from his south side home. Homicide Commander Joe DiLeonardi called the murder "an out and out assassination." Those who had designs for replacing Fort, soon forgot about such a grandiose scheme. Fort was in command for good.

I witnessed first hand the power Fort wielded over his troops. This was around late 1969 or early 1970. The Reverend John Fry, the pastor of a south side Presbyterian Church, had allowed the gang to have a sanctuary in the basement of one the church buildings. The police department suspected the gang had turned the facility into something of an arsenal.

I was there one afternoon with a film crew when a contingent of police officers surrounded the building. It appeared that the cops were going to storm the building and that there was going to be "blood on the moon." Needless to say it was a very tense situation.

However, Fort kept his troops "cool." The gang would pound their chests and shout "Stones" but that was all. Fort told his men that they would resist if the police came through the door but he ordered them not to start anything that would provoke the officers to use their weapons. After about a 45 minute standoff, that seemed forever, the police withdrew and we also beat a hasty retreat. There is no question, in my opinion, if Fort had not been in command, one of the Rangers quite easily could have triggered a shootout.

Fort went into voluntary exile in 1976 after his release from prison. It was in jail that he converted to Islam. After a short sojourn in Wisconsin he returned to Chicago and gathered his generals, or "emirs" as they were called, and announced that the Black P. Stone Nation was no more. He told his chieftains (his top subordinates were called the Main 21) that the gang would now be known as the El Rukns. Fort's new title was Chief King Malik while his top henchmen were given names like "Toomba," "Maumie," "Hassan," "Sabu," and other monikers too numerous to mention here.

The El Rukns claimed they were a religious organization of Moorish Americans, but skeptical law enforcement personnel described the group as a front for narcotics trafficking and other illegal activity. The drug allegations were substantiated in 1983 when Fort was indicted after a huge drug shipment was seized by federal authorities. Fort went back to jail.

At one time the imprisonment of a leader would mean that he was cut off from his gang and soon would lose much of his influence. He would no longer be able to have much say in the gang's day to day operation. But times had changed; incarceration no longer meant that the Boss was unable to call the shots while he did time.

Fort continued to rule and his set up was not that unique. Crime syndicate boss Joey "The Doves" Aiuppa was handed what amounted to a life sentence when he was convicted in Kansas City in 1987 in a Las Vegas skimming case. Yet Aiuppa, authorities said, continued to run the show from his prison cell for some time.

Fort gave his directives from a prison in Bastrop, Texas. He called almost daily to his confederates at the El Rukn temple. On some days Jeff would call the temple as many as ten times. The FBI recorded some 3,200 hours of phone conversations between the imprisoned Fort and his gang. Jeff was too crafty to put his cards on the table during those calls. Fearful that the FBI was listening, the El Rukn leader spoke in codes to his troops who were eager to hear their master's voice.

A veteran El Rukn general or emir, Trammel Davis, also known as "Tacu" or "Trim," helped the government de-code those calls. Davis was cooperating with the Justice Department after pleading guilty to racketeering and corruption charges. Fort was so obsessed about wiretaps that he gave the English language new meaning. Fortunately for investigators Davis was able to interpret what those vague terms meant. For example when Jeff talked about apples and oranges, he meant explosives. According to Davis, when Fort referred to "our young friend," he was referring to Libyan leader Moammar Gadhafi. A "Perry" was a lawyer—remember the television show, Perry Mason? When the El Rukn boss was talking about Miller Time or "Old Style," he wasn't talking about having a beer, he was referring to cocaine.

Here are a couple examples of those coded conversations. On November 5, 1985, Fort called collect from his prison in Texas. He talked to several of his associates, including the aforementioned Davis. In this conversation Fort was informed that one of his men had been shot by members of a rival gang, the Disciples.

"Tacu": Yes sir we drawing ah, them particularly one there. Yes sir, they, ah, they like ah, they liked touched 'em there."

Interpretation: The disciples shot him.

Fort: "Ah, heels?"

Interpretation: The Police?

"Tacu": "Ah, no sir. In the signs of them ah, little boys there."

Interpretation: No sir, the Disciples.

Later "Tacu," who is actually Trammel Davis, tells Fort that the police found out about the shooting and were canvassing the area.

"Tacu" : "And you know, the heels, they like, they like moving about there."

Interpretation: And you know the police are all around the area.

Fort: "Yeah."

"Tacu": "Yes, sir."

Fort: "The heels in tune with the, ah, particular ones, that, ah, drawed?"

Interpretation: Do the police know who the shooter is?

"Tacu": "We drawin that the, that the, ah, the little kids that live over there."

Interpretation: We think the kids in the area may have told.

Fort: "Yeah."

"Tacu": "They, they, they might might've mentioned it. They might've mentioned, ah ah, ah."

Interpretation: Told the police who did it.

Fort: "Day, day, day time demonstration?"

Interpretation: Did it happen during the daytime?

"Tacu": "Ah, no sir."

Fort: "Uh, huh."

"Tacu": Sun, sun, sundown.

Interpretation: It happened in the early evening.

In another call Fort is upset over a shipment of cocaine the El Rukns purchased and were trying to sell. Fort felt several of his generals had "screwed up" in getting a bad batch of coke.

El Rukn emir: "As a matter of fact, that demonstration there with, that they had manifested on the scene. That demonstration there was like ah, like ah, like a 40 watt demonstration."

Interpretation: As a matter of fact the cocaine, the cocaine they brought to Detroit, that cocaine was garbage.

Fort: "I see, yeah."

El Rukn emir: "And, ah, that, it was almost, sir, sir, the actual, the actual, ah, drawin. It was kinda like, the way, the way they brought it was kinda embarrassing, there sir."

Interpretation: The coke was so bad that I was embarrassed to be associated with (Fort names two subordinates).

Fort: "Uh, huh."

El Rukn emir: "Cause like that demonstration be, you know, it didn't even it didn't, you know."

Interpretation: The coke didn't even cook up.

Fort: "Right."

El Rukn general: "The watts was low."

Interpretation: It had too much mix on it.

Fort: "Right. Uh huh, I see."

El Rukn general: "But it."

Fort: "They had done a lot of things to that, you know."

Interpretation: They really diluted it, added a lot of mix to it.

Fort's plan of working the phones heavily eventually backfired. In 1987 U. S. District Judge Charles Norgle ruled that the El Rukn leader was in contempt of court for violating an order restricting him to one telephone call a day to his lawyer. The ruling came down after Fort had been transferred to the Metropolitan Correctional Center in Chicago. Fort was being held at the MCC where he was awaiting trial on charges that put him and the El Rukns in the international spotlight.

Two years before, while Fort was in prison on drug charges, several of his generals made contact with the Libyan government. The El Rukns supposedly were to receive $2.5 million from Libya in exchange for unleashing a terrorist campaign in the U.S. The terrorist acts would include the blowing up or burning of government buildings, army bases, and police stations.

The El Rukns evidently did meet with Libyan officials but there is no evidence that they had dealt directly with Libyan strongman Colonel Moammar Gadhafi. In the mid-1980s the Libyan leader and President Reagan were not on the best of terms. The relationship between Libya and the U.S. worsened in April, 1986, when Air Force F-3s conducted a raid on the Libyan capital of Tripoli. A number of Libyans were killed or wounded and damage was inflicted on Gadhafi's headquarters.

So when Fort and three of his associates were indicted in October, 1986 on conspiracy charges, the publics' worst fears were imagined. Did this mean a powerful street gang was in cahoots with America's enemies?

At the time of the indictment a Justice Department official said authorities felt it was not a serious attempt by the Libyan government to hire a street gang to carry out a reign of terror, but instead a ruse by the gang to obtain money.

Although Fort was in jail, he was nevertheless indicted of directing the plot because law enforcement officials contended he was calling the shots. Whether the El Rukns actually intended to carry out a terrorist plot is the subject of debate. However, there is no argument that the gang had amassed a cache of weapons. That gave credibility to the story that the El Rukns were going to commit terrorist acts at the behest of a foreign government.

Some of those weapons were seized when a large contingent of law enforcement personnel swooped down in a pre-dawn raid on an apartment building on Kenwood Avenue and at El Rukn headquarters on south Drexel Boulevard. At the El Rukn apartment the raiders hit the mother lode. A total of 37 firearms, including automatic weapons, three hand grenades, and an anti-tank gun were confiscated. The anti-tank gun or rocket had been sold to the gang by an FBI undercover agent who had posed as a black market arms dealer. The government said the anti-tank gun had been disarmed before it had been sold to the El Rukns. The raid on the fort, as the gang's headquarters on Drexel Boulevard was called, produced a quantity of cocaine and marijuana. Several firearms were also taken according to several reports.

ATF raid on El Rukn headquarters. WBBM-TV photo.

The government felt they now had the "goods" on Fort and his cronies. Despite protestations of innocence from Fort and his followers a jury found Jeff and four of his cohorts guilty in the terrorism-for-hire plot. They all received marathon prison sentences.

One of those indicted with Fort was not in the courtroom when the trial began. That was Melvin Mayes, known in gang circles as "Maumie." Mayes went on the lam and was the subject of an international manhunt, even being listed on the FBI's ten most wanted list. It took nine years to apprehend the El Rukn general who many believed had gone overseas. However, when Mayes was arrested it was on Indiana Avenue on Chicago's south side and not across the Atlantic. Mayes was later sentenced to prison but not before he renounced his U.S. citizenship, saying he was a citizen of "New Africa."

Melvin "Maumie" Mayes, an El Rukn leader, became a fugitive.

As far as Fort was concerned, his legal problems were far from over. In October, 1988 the El Rukn leaders and four of his high ranking henchmen were found guilty in Chicago of gunning down a street rival. The verdict was a body blow to the El Rukn hierarchy. The murder conviction, according to prosecutors, brought to 25 the number of El Rukn leaders convicted or sent to prison.

Fort was already in custody during the murder trial so there were no more scenes of Fort, wearing a Chinese Coolie hat and surrounded by bodyguards, leaving the courthouse. The scene of Jeff, his hat, and the El Rukn guards, had become a staple on the local TV newscasts during one of his earlier trials.

But other problems were looming for the gang. Their headquarters was soon to be a victim of a wrecking ball. Some law enforcement people believe they could put a nail in the coffin of the El Rukns if authorities demolished the El Rukn building on Drexel Boulevard.

Prior to the building's destruction I was invited by an El Rukn general to visit the facility and get the gang's view on recent events. I went there with a camera crew and sat with the Main 21, or what was left of that ruling body. Our meeting, if I recall correctly, took place on the second floor which had a stage and a big floor that resembled a dance hall. During our stay the leadership vigorously denied being involved in drug trafficking and contended the group was a religious organization which tried to do good things for the neighborhood. It was also said that El Rukn members did not use profanity and refrained from alcohol.

Our visit came after authorities had raided the building and the El Rukns wanted their day in court. I noticed, as I sat at a long table with the generals, that a throne-like seat, situated on a stage, was empty. That seat, I was told, belonged to Chief King Malik, a.k.a. Jeff Fort. The fort, as the gang referred to their headquarters, though was on its last legs.

In the fall of 1989 authorities seized the building and shut it down. A year later, amid lots of hoopla, the building was

Jeff Fort on the move, while being interviewed by Drummond.

razed as a 6,000 pound wrecking ball battered the old movie theater into submission. The event attracted a number of police officers, politicians, and dignitaries. One of the speakers was Mayor Daley. Other orators hailed the destruction of the building in what was termed a symbolic victory in the war on drugs.

With Fort serving a lengthy prison sentence, prosecutors turned their attention to some of his underlings. A number of El Rukn higher ups were convicted but many of those convictions were thrown out. That's because El Rukn members who had cooperated and were testifying for the government had been granted some favors that were "no nos." It was revealed that they were given drugs and received sexual favors from women visitors at the MCC.

The allegations of prosecutorial misconduct resulted in reduced sentences for 23 El Rukns who had been convicted earlier. Others were re-tried and most but not all were convicted again.

As to Jeff Fort, there is little likelihood that he will ever get out on prison. He was sentenced to an 80 year term on the terrorism for hire plot and then he was sentenced to 75 years in prison for the murder conviction. And those terms are to be served consecutively, not concurrently. That means when his 80 year hitch is finished, he will begin serving a 75 year term in a state institution for murder.

Fort, as of this writing, is being held at the Marion Federal Correctional Institution in southern Illinois. It's not a country club. His release date is May, 2044. At that time Jeff, if he is alive, will be 97 years old. How much influence Fort still has over his troops is unknown.

It's also unclear how much power the gang has over the community. By the way, the gang is longer called the El Rukns. The group once again is known as the Blackstone P. Nation. Whether the Stones, like the legendary Phoenix, can rise from the ashes is uncertain. But now they are no longer a force to be reckoned with.

14

STILL AMONG THE MISSING

An estimated 25,000 persons are reported missing in the Chicago area each year. That sounds incredible, but that figure does not mean that the vast majority of those reported missing met with foul play or simply vanished.

Many of those cases involve juveniles who have run away and eventually come home. The same can be said of angry spouses who take off following a family dispute and then after a cooling off period return to the household, a bit repentant. Then there are the cases of elderly persons who wander off from a nursing home or extended care facility. They usually turn up, although some after wandering aimlessly, succumb to severe weather conditions or are fatally stuck by a car or truck. Thus, most missing persons cases are solved routinely with little fanfare. The success rate in clearing the average disappearance affair is quite high. But there are some scenarios that to this day, still baffle police.

One that fits that category, is the disappearance of one Woodruff Scovil Kelly, Jr., known to his associates and friends as Woody. I profiled the Kelly story in my earlier book, *Thirty Years in the Trenches*, but even though there have been no major developments regarding Kelly in recent years, I felt the Kelly saga is worthy of another mention.

Woody Kelly was a hail fellow well met type who could charm the pants off of a potential investor if he wanted to.

Woodruff Scovil Kelly, Jr. aka "Woody."
One of Lake County's biggest mysteries.

Kelly would tell strangers and clients alike, "Call me Woody." Kelly liked the good life—a Mercedes automobile, a lakeside mansion, and a yacht. Woody, at least on the surface, appeared to have it all.

Kelly was an investment counselor from Antioch, Illinois, a small community in the Chicago metro area. Woody had a persona about him that folks were attracted to on first contact. The only trouble, according to Uncle Sam, was that Woody defrauded some 300 investors. In fact, one investor alleged that his family had lost $483,000 that it had entrusted to Kelly. Most of these folks, who allegedly had been swindled by Woody, would have loved to catch up with Kelly and wreak vengeance on him. But that never happened as Woody vanished as the authorities were closing in on him. The Justice Department indicted Woody on mail fraud charges and the Antioch businessman was declared a fugitive by the FBI.

Mark Schoenfield, who once represented an insurance company involved in the case, said Kelly had reason to vamoose. Schoenfield told me, "There were a lot of angry people sore at Woody." And Schoenfield added another possible motive for his disappearance, "Law enforcement people had what is known in the trade as a slam dunk for the prosecution side."

Woody Kelly vanished on June 8, 1985, after taking his 42 foot cabin cruiser Piscator out onto Lake Michigan for a trial run. The next day Kelly's boat was spotted drifting close to short near Winthrop Harbor, Illinois. When authorities beached the boat they found no trace of Woody. Could the Antioch businessman, who suffered from high blood pressure, perhaps gotten dizzy and fallen off the Piscator? It's possible but very unlikely. Coast Guard figures show that the vast bulk of drowning victims in Lake Michigan are eventually recovered. The body of Woody Kelly has never been found in the lake. That does not rule out the possibility that he could have fallen off the boat, but it's a long shot.

The water, the day Kelly disappeared, was quite calm by Lake Michigan standards, and Kelly was an experienced sailor, no novice when it came to operating a boat. Then there was the matter of the briefcase. A witness said he saw Kelly boarding the boat carrying a brief case. No brief case was ever found. Also, two people claimed to have seen Woody since his disappearance. A Lake County sheriff's policeman said he saw Kelly at the Busch Gardens Amusement Park in Florida. Another man, a firefighter, said he saw the missing man driving a luxury car in Waukegan.

Kelly's disappearance touched off a media blitz. He was even featured on *America's Most Wanted*, but nothing came of it. Area television stations and newspapers gave the Kelly case plenty of coverage, but the publicity did not garner any leads.

Seven years after Kelly took his cabin cruiser for a run in the lake, Woody's former wife Ann Proctor asked a Lake County judge to declare her ex-spouse legally dead. If the judge decided that Kelly was indeed dead it would have meant that Proctor and her three children would have been able to collect some $450,000 in life insurance. But the request came to naught when the judge denied the family request. The jurist apparently felt there was no evidence that Kelly was deceased.

It's been over 20 years since Woody disappeared and there have been no recent sightings of him. And area investors continue to wonder, not just about Kelly, but also about some $6,000,000 of their money that is also missing.

Loretta "Lori" Guinan grew up a on a farm near the small town of Boscobel in southwest Wisconsin. Lori, as her friends called her, was not content to be just the farmer's daughter and at the age of 17, and just out of high school, she moved to Chicago where the lifestyle was light years away from tiny Boscobel.

Lori's friend, Deborah Arneson, said that although Lori was a beautiful girl she was, "very shy, quite innocent, and very naive." She soon met lawyer Michael Guinan, 22 years her senior. Guinan was a successful criminal lawyer who specialized in narcotics cases. Guinan had some big time clients

Loretta "Lori" Guinan vanished from her apartment. U.S. Marshal's photo.

in that field including the notorious Herrerra drug family of heroin fame. Guinan, because of his clientele, was called in some circles the "Mexican Mouthpiece."

According to Arneson, Lori was out hitchhiking one day and Guinan picked her up. Before long Lori became Guinan's mistress and soon Mike divorced his first wife and in January, 1984 Lori and Michael were married. According to government documents the two apparently lived high off the hog prior to their marriage. The documents further state that Michael and Loretta traveled extensively from 1977 to 1982, usually in Florida and the Caribbean. The same government motion alleges that during 1977 and 1978, the two took approximately twelve trips each year with each sojourn lasting from four to seven days. During 1979 the couple took a long fling, island hopping in the Caribbean. The trips were paid for in cash. Cash was used to pay for air fare, lodging, meals, gambling, and other expenses that totaled tens of thousands of dollars. In other words the two of them were real jet setters with money to burn.

But after the couple was married in January, 1984, the wedding bliss didn't last very long. The marriage went on the rocks and Lori moved out of the couple's condo in fashionable Lake Point Tower and into a near north side apartment.

Meanwhile the free wheeling Guinan had been under scrutiny by the IRS. Uncle Sam contended that the LaSalle Street lawyer spent more than $1,000,000 from 1977 to 1980 but understated his income and was involved in several dubious financial deals. It appeared that Guinan had reported far less income than he had earned in those four years. It wasn't a penny ante amount either; it was nearly $300,000. The feds called it tax fraud and a December, 1984, trial date was set for Guinan.

Loretta soon got into the act. When she found out that Uncle Sam was zeroing in on her estranged husband she voluntarily contacted the government and offered to testify. Lori did appear before a grand jury and had numerous meetings with IRS agents, the last of which was on November 2, 1984. She had been promised immunity and would have been a key witness for the government in the case against her ex-spouse. Authorities were concerned about her well being but Lori refused an offer of protection and did not want to enter the witness protection program. Government sleuths last met with Lori shortly before the 27 year old woman was scheduled to meet Guinan so that she could retrieve some personal belongings from his apartment. On November 6, 1984, Lori Guinan disappeared. A government motion states "that her near north side apartment and personal belongings were found to be essentially intact." When a friend became worried later in the week of November 4th, she entered the apartment and found food spoiling on the stove and in the refrigerator.

Former U.S. Representative Barry Goldwater, Jr., the son of the onetime presidential nominee Barry Goldwater, was romantically involved with the blonde Loretta. He testified at Guinan's trial that he had spoken to Mrs. Guinan on the phone on November 5th. Goldwater told the court "It was obvious she was scared and didn't know what to do." According to Goldwater, Lori agreed to meet him the next day. But Goldwater said on the stand, "That's the last I ever heard from her."

U.S. Marshals and Chicago police detectives spent hundred of hours investigating her disappearance and attempting to learn Lori's whereabouts. Despite the intensive search, sleuths were unable to determine what had happened to the missing woman. Meanwhile Michael Guinan was scheduled to go on trial in December, 1984. However, on the eve of his trial Guinan fled and became a fugitive, although not before he withdrew $12,000 from a Chicago bank.

Guinan became the object of a nationwide manhunt until he was arrested in San Diego in April, 1985, some four months after his vanishing act. Mike led the lawmen on a merry chase with pit stops in Florida, Oklahoma City, Phoenix, suburban Chicago, and finally near San Diego where he was apprehended. When he was picked up in California the fugitive had in his possession two firearms and a quantity of ammunition. He also had in his possession a telephone recording cassette tape taken from Lori Guinan's apartment. Guinan was brought back to Chicago to face the music in a trial that began in July, 1985.

When the government had its day in court, Prosecutor Joe Duffy charged that Guinan had used more than three dozen bank accounts and a rash of aliases and safe deposit boxes to

Michael Guinan, surrounded by Marshals after his capture in California. WBBM-TV photo.

avoid paying federal income taxes. Lori Guinan's grand jury testimony was also entered which helped to bolster the government's case. There was little doubt as to the outcome. Duffy and his co-counsel, Thomas Durkin, had presented a strong case. Guinan was convicted and sentenced to a 16 year jail term.

Guinan, though did not find the Sandstone Federal Correctional Facility in northern Minnesota to his liking. He escaped from the medium security institution, but was soon apprehended and a year and a half was tacked onto his prison term.

Although Guinan was a suspect in his wife's disappearance he could not or would not shed any light in the matter. Michael Guinan, a onetime football star at Mt. Carmel High School was released from prison and died in 2003. If Guinan knew what had happened to Lori he carried the secret to his grave.

Jim Tantillo, a former member of the Marshal's Service spearheaded efforts to find Lori. Remains of women, approximately of Lori's age were found in Kankakee, Illinois, Kansas City, Missouri, and Crown Point, Indiana . However, none was Mrs. Guinan. Investigators connected to the Guinan investigation are all convinced that she met with foul play. They feel she was murdered.

As we indicated earlier most missing children soon turn up. Many juveniles simply run away but come back after they find that the grass on the other side is not automatically greener. Then there are missing children who are involved in a custody dispute between estranged or divorced parents. They are usually located by private investigators retained by one of the parents.

But that has not been the case of the two south side sisters, who disappeared from their neighborhood on July 6, 2001. The two young girls are the Bradley sisters, ten year old Tionda and three year old Diamond. Their case attracted massive media attention and became a national story.

The search for the two girls has been exhaustive and as of this writing a $30,000 reward has been offered for the person who finds the Bradley girls. Authorities are convinced that the Bradley sisters did not wander off on their own. Speculation has been rampant as to the girls' fate with theories ranging from abduction by a serial killer to a kidnaper who snatched the sisters and went overseas with them.

Chicago Police have looked at every nook and cranny in the girls' neighborhood, including basements, abandoned buildings, parks, and garbage dumps, but to no avail. Tips have come into the police saying the girls were spotted in Wisconsin, Mississippi, and even North Africa. Unfortunately, nothing substantial has come from that information.

In 2004 the National Center For Missing And Exploited Children posted age progression photos on its web site to indicate how the girls would look if they were still alive. Advances in forensic technology have helped authorities to depict how a missing child has aged.

Technological wizardry is a great tool, but in the Bradley sisters' case it has produced no results. The missing Bradley sisters have received A-1 priority from police but investigators apparently are at a dead end.

Unlike the Bradley sisters, law enforcement believes it knows what happened to Barbara Glueckert. Glueckert was a 14 year old Mt. Prospect girl when she disappeared after attending a rock concert near Huntley, Illinois on August 21, 1976. Barbara was the daughter of Robert Glueckert, a well known northwest suburban businessman.

In trying to re-trace Barbara's steps before she vanished, detectives believe she had attended five o'clock mass at a church in Mt. Prospect and then went to a pizza parlor with a girl friend. It was there the two teenagers met a young man who identified himself as Tom Edwards. Edwards convinced the two girls to accompany him to the rock concert. Edwards,

Missing suburban girl, Barbara Glueckert. . Mt. Prospect P.D. photo.

according to police, was 24 year old Thomas Urlacher, who had his share of run-ins with the police.

After Barbara disappeared Urlacher said he didn't know what became of her after he had dropped her off at a party that night. In fact Urlacher hi-tailed it out of the Chicago area the night Barbara disappeared. He ended up on the west coast where in December, 1974, four months after the teenage girl vanished, Urlacher wrote an incriminating letter to a friend, who was living in Illinois at the time. The friend, rather than destroying the letter as Urlacher had requested, turned it over to police.

The letter is an actual confession, as Urlacher wrote, "I put that girl in the ground because I was afraid she was going to tell the law I made her get me off."

Urlacher was returned to Illinois but no grand jury indictment was returned. Urlacher contended he was under the influence of drugs when he wrote the latter and didn't know what he was saying. No murder indictment was ever returned in the case since prosecutors felt, that because they had no body, a conviction was very unlikely.

However a similar problem did not stop prosecutors from gaining guilty verdicts in the cases of Palatine housewife Stephanie Lyng and a young Chicago woman, Marci Andrews. In both instances juries bought the state's arguments despite the absence of a corpus delicti.

The Glueckert family did go the civil suit route against Urlacher and were awarded $5.15 million by a jury in 1981, but reportedly Urlacher never paid a dime to the Glueckerts.

Urlacher, feeling that the Chicago area was too hot for him, moved to Oregon, where he worked as a lumberjack. It was there in Astoria, Oregon, that authorities said he raped an 18 year old girl, who like Barbara Glueckert had accepted a ride with him. However, in an ensuing trial Urlacher was found not guilty of first degree rape.

But Urlacher had a penchant for getting into trouble. He moved to Colorado where between 1993 and 2001 he was arrested 14 times for charges ranging from arson to food stamp fraud. In some ways Urlacher led a charmed life, skating from being the prime suspect in a high profile murder to an acquittal on a rape charge. Urlacher's luck finally ran out in the spring of 2005 when he was shot to death in Pueblo, Colorado, in a drug deal gone bad. Pueblo police found the former Illinoisan lying in a patch of bushes, the victim of five gunshot wounds.

The death of Urlacher has not deterred Mt. Prospect Police from trying to find Barbara's remains. There have been a number of searches but no trace of the missing girl has been found. At one point investigators were hopeful the mystery had been solved. An Elgin couple, who were fishing on August 22, 1976, the day after Barbara had disappeared, told authorities that they thought they heard someone digging nearby. A dig uncovered some bones but it turned out the bones were from an animal and were not from a human. Another dig in September of 2006 at a different location in St. Charles Township, west of Chicago was also unproductive.

One of the Mt. Prospect detectives working on the Glueckert case is Mike Nelson, who has a strong motive in pursuing the matter. Nelson, you see, went to grade school with Barbara and will not throw in the towel until Barbara's body is found, giving some semblance of closure to the Glueckert family.

The list of missing person cases is seemingly endless. Here are just several of them that still baffle police.

In August, 1998 a restaurateur from Morton Grove, Enrico Sylva closed his eatery for the night and has never been seen since.

In October of 1970, 36 year old Maria Tracz, a mother of three, disappeared. Her locked van was found in a shopping mall without any sign of a struggle. Police suspect foul play.

In June, 1981, Sal Pullia, a Proviso Township Committeeman and a rising star in the Democratic Party vanished. The 33 year old Pullia was last seen leaving a drive-in restaurant just two blocks from his Melrose Park home. Pullia has never been seen since. Federal investigators believe he was abducted and killed by the mob.

The reader may well wonder whey we did not give priority to the disappearance of candy heiress Helen Vorhees in this chapter. That's because many people don't believe it's a mystery anymore. Mrs. Brach, as many of our readers remember, vanished from her suburban Glenview home in February of 1977 (also see pages 39-40). Mrs. Brach, the widow of candy magnate Frank Brach, was the wealthiest woman to have ever disappeared.

Even though authorities say the Brach case is still open, several investigators from the ATF and some former prosecutors say the case has been solved. In 2005 it was revealed that a middle aged horseman, Joe Plemmons, had spilled his guts to ATF agent John Rotunno, who has been investigating the Brach mystery for years.

According to Plemmons, and Rotunno believes he's credible, Brach was severely beaten in her Glenview home and then transported to a south suburban stable owned by one Kenneth Hansen. Hansen, an unscrupulous horseman, was convicted of murdering three young boys back in 1955. But at the time of the Brach incident, justice had not yet caught up with him.

According to Plemmons, a car containing Brach was brought to the stables. Plemmons says that when the trunk was opened, Mrs. Brach although beaten badly was still alive. Plemmons contends he was given a revolver by Hansen's brother, Curt and ordered to shoot the woman. Plemmons says he had no choice but to comply or he would have been killed by Curt Hansen for not following orders. Curt Hansen was a reputed mob enforcer who died of natural causes in 1993. We are not naming the other individuals allegedly involved because they have not been charged.

Plemmons says Mrs. Brach's body was driven to a steel mill in northwest Indiana where it was placed in a blast furnace and the remains were literally evaporated.

Cook County authorities have not charged anybody in the Brach case because, they say, Plemmons story cannot be corroborated. Also they say that Plemmons' track record is not that of a choir boy and defense attorneys would have a field day when Joe took the stand.

You may have heard the term, vanished without a trace, that police are baffled and investigators are stumped. Such terminology fits the bill in the disappearance of an Arlington Heights couple who disappeared on May 15, 1970.

Edward Andrews and his wife Stephania were seen leaving a cocktail party at a Michigan Avenue hostelry, the former Sheraton Chicago hotel. We know this: the couple left the party at about 9:30 P.M. and took the elevator to an underground parking facility. Witnesses told police that Edward Andrews was staggering as he walked toward his 1969

Oldsmobile. Parking garage employees told detectives that Stephanie Andrews was crying and urged her husband not to drive home. But apparently she was unable to dissuade her husband from getting behind the wheel.

The last anybody ever saw of the Andrews was when their car sped out of the garage and turned south on the lower level of Michigan Avenue. What happened next is theory and conjecture.

Authorities believe Andrews became confused behind the wheel and realized he was going south in the northbound lanes of lower Michigan Avenue. At that point police believe he may have attempted a U-turn but drove into the Chicago river at a location where there were no guard rails. The area where the car may have plunged into the river was searched and dragged but no trace of the car or its occupants were found.

Arlington Heights Police Captain Michael Schenkel told me that what he called extensive searches were made in the Chicago River but again nothing concerning the couple ever turned up. It seems incredible that divers, boats, and helicopters were unable to provide any clues as to the whereabouts of the couple.

Then in 1994, an informant told police that the Andrews had been murdered and their bodies stuffed in the trunk of the Oldsmobile. According to the informant the car was then sunk in a Lake County pond off the Illinois Tollway. Divers checked out the pond and found no car or any human remains. Although authorities felt they had been had, police say they had no alternative but to check out the story even though it turned out to be a wild goose chase.

The Andrews mystery is over 36 years old and police are no closer to solving it than they were that May night in 1970 when the Arlington Heights couple fell off the face of the earth.

15

THE GERIATRIC GANGSTER

He was the only Chicago mobster to admit under oath that he had been involved in six murders and yet he never did any time for those slayings. He was one of the highest ranking members of the Chicago Outfit to co-operate with the government and with the possible exception of Jake Guzik and Ralph Pierce, was the foremost Jewish mobster in the history of the Chicago Crime Syndicate.

Lenny Patrick admitted to several gangland slayings. Chicago Crime Commission photo.

That was Lenny Patrick, the longtime boss of the Lawndale and Rogers Park neighborhoods in the city. Patrick was no suave, polished gangster. He came out of a then Jewish ghetto on the city's west side, a tough kid with a chip on his shoulder. Patrick, who was raised in an orphanage, entered manhood as the Depression was getting into high gear. Like many of his mob contemporaries Patrick had only a limited education. Seventh grade was as high as he got and there weren't many employment opportunities for a youth with few job skills, so he turned to crime.

According to accounts, 24th Ward powerhouse Arthur Elrod used the youthful and husky Patrick on election days to make sure the ballot boxes were stuffed with the names of organization candidates. Patrick was a stocky 200 pounder who could turn on the muscle when his superiors wanted him to.

In 1932, 19 year old Patrick encountered his first serious joust with the law. He was indicted for the murder of one Herman Glick. Glick, as the story went, had worked over Lenny in a fight so Patrick shot him in the back and head about a week later. Glick became the first of a number of victims who had crossed swords with Lenny. But nothing ever came of the incident and Lenny skated.

As a youth Patrick had a wild and vicious side. Bank jobs and violent heists were part of Patrick's curriculum. Using the nom de guerre of Joe Cohen, Patrick pulled a bank job in the town of Culver, Indiana, a community that became well known because of the military academy located there. But Patrick got caught soon after the robbery when his getaway car ran out of gas. This time Patrick spent almost seven years in the Indiana State Prison in Michigan City.

The stretch in the Indiana State pen must have wised Lenny up. He realized there must be other and better ways to make a buck. Not that Patrick went legit. He remained an underworld figure, soon using his reputation as a mob heavy to cut a swath in Chicago's criminal community. No more bank jobs or stick ups for Lenny. The Outfit realized they could use this up and coming hoodlum for muscle as an enforcer.

Patrick was pretty much of an unknown as far as the media was concerned until 1946. That's when James Ragen, the owner of Continental Press, a racetrack wire service, was murdered. The Outfit operated a rival race results service, called Trans-America, and the Syndicate wanted Ragen to either sell out or pay a substantial tribute to them each month. It was a new version of the old protection racket.

Ragen, a tough Irishman, wouldn't back down even though he realized he had antagonized a formidable foe. He hired his own bodyguards, but he was doomed.

On June 24, 1946, while driving his own car on the south side he was ambushed by three men. His bodyguards were in a chase car but they were too late to save their boss.

In a scene resembling a B-Movie, a delivery truck, covered with a tarpaulin, pulled alongside Ragen's car, with its occupants blasting away with shotguns. Ragen's bodyguards fired at the speeding truck; however, the killers got away.

Ragen, seriously wounded, was rushed to Michael Reese Hospital where, after undergoing surgery, he appeared on the road to recovery. Then Ragen's kidneys began to fail and he underwent surgery again, only this time he died four days later. An autopsy was performed and it revealed that Ragan had been poisoned. The Outfit had apparently bribed somebody on the hospital staff to make sure that Ragen would never be a problem anymore. The poisoning incident sent a chilling message. If a patient in a hospital, who had some kind of protection, could be harmed, then nobody who crossed the Outfit was safe.

The Ragen murder caused an uproar, but despite a public outcry nobody was put in the dock. Patrick and two other gunsels, William Black and Dave Yaras, were indicted; however that was as far as it got. The state thought it had a strong case with three eye witnesses. The case, though soon began to unravel when the star witness changed his testimony and the statements of the other two witnesses were thrown out. That was par for the course in that era. Charges were filed in Outfit murder cases but nobody was ever convicted.

Patrick soon became a force to be reckoned with. He was the Mob's gambling and vice czar in the Lawndale neighborhood although the ethnic composition of that area was

An older Lenny Patrick, the feared mob gambling boss.

changing from Jewish to black. For a while though Lenny held sway, keeping residents toeing the line. In fact Lenny was calling the shots there until the mid 1960s. It was in that period that Patrick's name surfaced again, this time in another murder investigation.

That was when 24th Ward Alderman Ben Lewis was found handcuffed and lying in a pool of blood in his office on a winter morning in 1963. Lewis was a onetime Georgia farmboy and CTA bus driver who became the first black to represent the 24th Ward in the City Council. Lewis, to put it mildly, had a flamboyant lifestyle, and even though there was a multitude of publicity and a $10,000 reward the murder was never solved.

Was Patrick involved? We may never know although street talk said that Lewis owed money to Syndicate gamblers and was welching on the debt. As one story went, the killer was a 325 pound ex-heavyweight boxer who was employed by the Outfit as an enforcer. The former fighter was questioned but never charged and to this day the Lewis murder remains open. As a footnote, Lewis was the first and last alderman to have been murdered while in office.

Times were changing and even with the menacing Patrick on board, the mob was losing control of its fiefdom on the west side. The black street gangs were getting more powerful so Patrick exited his old domain and moved his operation to the Rogers Park neighborhood on the north side. Anything north of Touhy Avenue was Patrick's turf. Bill Lambie, the former operating director of the Chicago Crime Commission, described Patrick's role for the Mob then as "something of a district manager."

Those were the halcyon days for Lenny. In the 1960s everything turned up roses for Patrick. In Rogers Park, Albany Park, Lincolnwood, and other north side areas, he was the Mob's guy. Authorities said that Lenny was an expert when it came to running a gambling operation or shaking down some poor businessman who was vulnerable to the Outfit's overtures. You could find Lenny most every night playing the role at a far north side steakhouse. Yes, Patrick had it made in those days.

But in 1975 Patrick's ride on easy street came to an end, albeit a temporary one. He was held in civil contempt by Federal Judge Prentice Marshall when he refused to testify in a tax fraud trial of a Chicago Police lieutenant. According to the government, Patrick made payoffs to the policeman so that his gambling venture wouldn't be raided by the cops. The Police lieutenant was charged with failing to report more than $65,00 dollars on his tax returns, bribe money he allegedly received from Patrick.

But when Patrick got on the witness stand at the trial, his memory failed him, even though he had been granted immunity from prosecution. Patrick gave his name and address and that was about it. When Prosecutor James Henderson asked Patrick a question, he invoked the Fifth Amendment and read

Patrick being led to car by FBI agents. WBBM-TV photo.

the Fifth Amendment privilege from a file card each and every time he was questioned. Without Patrick's testimony the lieutenant was acquitted. An angry Judge Marshall ordered Patrick into the custody of U.S. Marshals and criminal contempt charges were brought against the north side Mob boss. That meant Patrick would be facing a trial for his failure to cooperate.

In September, 1975, a federal jury deliberated less than an hour before finding Patrick guilty. Then in October, a stern-faced Judge Marshall gave Lenny a tongue lashing saying, "Patrick has used the judicial system for his own purpose and not suffered the consequences....I sentence you to four years in the penitentiary."

Patrick didn't throw in the towel and meekly march off to prison. His lawyer filed a last ditch appeal contending that his client suffered from severe psychoneurosis, chronic anxiety, and extreme depression. Such a problem, Lenny's defense team contended, gave him suicidal thoughts. And there was more, Patrick was portrayed as a model citizen or close to it. Lawyers wrote that Patrick "was a compassionate man who pays medical bills of strangers, takes home stray dogs, and whose humanity for others is boundless." Judge Marshall wouldn't budge and upheld Patrick's prison sentence, although he did serve his time at the Federal prison in Lexington, Kentucky, one of the better places to be incarcerated in the 1970s.

Leonard Patrick was in his mid 60s when he entered prison and when he got out his criminal career would seem to be over. When Patrick was released from Lexington, lawmen assumed Lenny would go the pipe and slippers route. Nothing could have been farther from the truth. He was more than just an ordinary pensioner. Soon there was street talk that, in the middle and late 1980s, Patrick was into some mischief again.

It turned out to be more than just street talk because on December 18, 1991, a federal grand jury indicted the mob's connection man, Gus Alex, Patrick, and two confederates of extorting some $376,000 from legitimate businessmen. Alex, known to his colleagues as "Slim", was a major domo in the Outfit. He was the Mob's liaison with crooked judges, businessmen, labor leaders, and other who did the Syndicate's bidding. In 1965 he succeeded the legendary Murray "The Camel" Humphreys when the Welshman succumbed to a fatal heart attack in his Marina City apartment.

Although Alex epitomized "class" for the Mob, he was no shrinking violet. He had an arrest record dating back to the early 1930s and was a suspect in a number of murders and assaults, although he was never convicted of any of them. Gus had a swank apartment on Lake Shore Drive and was seen in his heyday in the best Chicago restaurants and nightclubs. Yet he thumbed his nose at the Justice Department and the Senate for that matter, taking the Fifth 39 times before the McClellan Committee.

A sidebar about these old timers: both of these men were paranoid about getting their pictures taken by the media,

Gus Alex—They called him "Slim," and he knew the right people.

Patrick in particular. I remember waiting, back in 1975, along with cameraman George Case, in the federal building lobby for Patrick to come downstairs. We were hiding behind a pillar and as soon as Patrick spotted us, he quickly put a handkerchief over his face. Then when he was indicted in 1991, Assignment Editor Ed Marshall sent cameraman Dino Pillizzi to Patrick's northwest side home. As luck would have it Patrick was being taken out of his house by two FBI agents shortly after the cameraman arrived. Patrick began weaving and bobbing in an effort to prevent Pillizzi from getting a good shot. In fact, Patrick resembled "Willie the Wisp" Pep, a former featherweight boxing champion, who was a master at bobbing and weaving. Despite Patrick's efforts Pillizzi got excellent tape of the aging mobster. Alex was also old school. When he was brought in to testify before a Florida grand jury investigating the murder of John Roselli, Miami TV station

WTVJ was on hand but when Alex spotted the TV crew he also covered his face with a handkerchief. However, by 1992 the aging and ailing Alex was too infirm to play any shenanigans with photographers in the lobby of the Dirksen Federal Building.

Prosecutors were excited about charges against Alex. After all he was a big fish in a big pond. Patrick was no piker either. He had been around a long, long time and if he would talk what stories he could tell. And that's what happened. Lenny Patrick in April, 1992, not only pleaded guilty to racketeering charges but also agreed to testify against co-defendant Gus Alex. This was Outfit history, the aging Patrick becoming the foremost mobster to ever defect. Patrick's lawyer, David Mejia, explained Lenny's guilty plea, saying the longtime hoodlum had a heart condition and didn't want to die in prison.

The newspaper and television reporters were salivating at the thought that the two septuagenarian mobsters would face off in court. Alex was 76 and Patrick 78 at the time. The late Bill Roemer, a retired FBI agent and author about the Mob, compared the face off to the Muhammad Ali-George Foreman "rumble in the jungle" in 1974. Only Roemer said the Patrick-Alex match should be described as the "rumble in the asphalt jungle."

The Patrick-Alex imbroglio continued to grab headlines well before the trial got underway. It was revealed that Patrick had worn a wire and had tape recorded conversations with his former boss and at least one of the other defendants. About a month after word had gotten out about Patrick's role as a defector, a car parked outside his daughter Sharon's West Roger Park home was bombed. No one was injured but the blast shattered windows in at least four houses and left a driveway crater five inches deep and two feet across. It didn't take a Rhodes Scholar to figure out that the bombing was meant as a message to Patrick to keep quiet. A parade of Mob figures

Patrick in car with handkerchief over his face. WBBM-TV photo.

was called to the Dirksen Federal Building to appear before a grand jury. But the mobsters wouldn't or couldn't shed any light on the incident. Alex's attorney Carl Walsh told reporters that his client had nothing to do with the bombing. As far as Patrick was concerned, he didn't budge and he went ahead and testified.

A different kind of bombshell was dropped in Federal Court when Prosecutor Chris Gair told Judge James Alesia that Patrick was offered $100,000 if he kept his mouth shut and not testify, In other words Lenny was to get temporary amnesia.

To add fuel to the fire, Patrick took the stand in a pre-trial hearing and said he had received a message from Alex through Lenny's lawyer, that he was threatened with death if he kept singing. It was never satisfactorily explained if the threat and Alex's offer were real. But the allegations did not put a halt to the trial.

Neither did allegations by Alex's attorneys that Gus was incompetent and unfit to stand trial. The Judge vetoed that notion and the much awaited affair got underway in the fall of 1992. Alex, who was free on bond, didn't appear to be a Syndicate wheelhorse as he entered the courthouse for jury selection. Alex, the Outfit's connection man, was a frail looking gentlemen as he shuffled slowly through the lobby with a cane in one hand and either a relative or one of his lawyers holding him up on the other side. He seemed a bit confused but cynics said that was all part of an act to get sympathy from the jury. Federal authorities said at the time that Alex might look frail and weak but he was a high ranking Crime Syndicate figure, a political fixer, and an extortionist.

As prosecutors outlined their case, they contended that Alex was the actual boss of the operation and that the Lenny Patrick street crew did the actual dirty work. The Patrick crew used death threats, beatings, and, in one instance, an attempted fire bombing to intimidate their victims. The victims, by the way, were not down and out horseplayers. They were prominent restaurant proprietors, car dealers and in the case of the fire bombing, a theater owner. The crew garnered close to $400,000 in extortion payments. Patrick personally collected a $150,000 payment from a suburban Niles car dealer. Lawmen, journalists, and Mob buffs who thought the old protection racket was a throwback to the Prohibition era were in for a rude awakening.

Two of Patrick's henchmen, Mario Rainone and Nick Gio were indicted by the grand jury in the case. But Rainone pleaded guilty and never went to trial. A third enforcer James La Valley decided to go the straight and narrow route and cooperated with the government.

Prosecutor Gair described Alex as the Chairman of the Board, the man Patrick had get approval from for the shakedowns. Patrick, who was the "Bell Cow" in the government's case, put on quite a show when he took the stand in a packed

Dirksen Building courtroom. There was one thing both the prosecution and the defense agreed on, is that the testimony of Patrick was pivotal to the case.

D-Day was September 16, 1992. It was the Federal Buildings' version of the gunfight at the O.K. Corral with two members of the social security set squaring off. Prosecutors knew they didn't have a Mr. Rogers on the stand so to diffuse defense attempts to show Patrick's violent past they laid Lenny's cards on the table. Patrick broke 60 years of silence, telling of murders that he had been involved in. The box score, six homicides, including two in which Patrick was the actual triggerman:

Herman Glick, April 4, 1932

Willie Kalatsch, April 6, 1945

Harry Krotish, AKA Harry the Horse, Dec.10, 1947

David Zatz, May 6, 1952

Milton Glickman, January 4, 1953

Edward Murphy, March 22, 1960

Explaining the slaying of Murphy, his old partner, Patrick said, "He wanted to take over. It was either him or me. That's the way it went."

The aforementioned victims were mostly bookies or gamblers and Patrick did not own up to several higher publicized slayings. In his courtroom confession Patrick said nothing about the murders of James Ragen, Police Captain William Drury, or Alderman Ben Lewis. Patrick's name had surfaced in all of those homicides.

After rattling off those six earlier misdeeds, Patrick got down to the meat of the government's case against Alex. Patrick said he first met Alex in the 1950s. Some 30 years later, Patrick testified, he was working for Alex. Patrick said he needed Alex's permission before Lenny and his thugs could put the arm on restaurant owners, car dealers and other legitimate businessmen. When he got Alex's okay, Patrick testified,

Alex would caution him by saying "Go ahead, but be careful." Patrick told the jury that he would meet with Alex once or twice a week to give Gus his share of the Patrick crew's profits.

Patrick testified that to avoid surveillance by law enforcement the two men would get together in a place like Northwestern Memorial Hospital or the big department store Marshall Field's where Patrick claimed he would hand over Alex's cut of the shakedown proceeds. But unknown to Alex, Patrick had been cooperating with the government and in several of those meetings Lenny was wearing a wire. In a December 4, 1989, confab at the hospital, Patrick is heard on tape giving Alex a good chunk of cash. The tape made points with the jury.

Alex had two capable attorneys, Carl Walsh, a longtime barrister for Tony Accardo, and Sam Adam, a veteran of the Criminal Courts Building. Adam had indicated in his opening statement that the government's case would stand or fall on the testimony of Lenny Patrick. And when he started cross examining the prosecution's star witness the fireworks began.

Adam going for the jugular: "You're testifying here so you don't have to go to jail?"

Patrick: "That's about it." Asked about the six murders Patrick replied, "I done it to protect myself. I don't shoot anybody for the fun of it." At one point Patrick blurted out, "You're trying to bury me. They're no saints in this room."

Adams asked Patrick, if in addition to the six murders he had testified to, if he had killed anybody else. Patrick replied sarcastically. "I've run out of cemeteries." The gallery guffawed periodically during the cross; it was after all some of the best courtroom theater anybody had ever seen.

Adam asked Patrick about the extortion of Ray Hara, the owner of a car dealership in suburban Niles. Patrick said he had tried to shakedown Hara for $300,000, but settled for

$150,000. The breakdown, according to Patrick—75 thousand for Alex, 37.5 thousand for Patrick, and 37.5 to be split among members of Patrick's crew. Explained Patrick: "I gave him (Hara) a break. I cut it in half; I'm proud of myself." That comment drew raucous laughter from the spectators.

The defense counsel moved on, grilling Patrick about his clashes with lawmen and grand juries.

Adam: "In the past when you have come into contact with law enforcement authorities have you been truthful with them?"

Patrick: "No, I haven't."

Adam: "And when you say you haven't been truthful with them, have you lied to FBI agents in the past?"

Patrick: "Yes, I did."

Later Adam asked Lenny about his grand jury experiences.

Adam: "Do you remember telling the grand jury back in 1974 that you quit bookmaking when the new Federal Book-making Illegal Gambling Business law was passed in 1970?"

Patrick: "Yes I did."

Adam: "True or false?"

Patrick: "False."

And so it went. Patrick admitted he had lied in the past but insisted he was telling the truth about Gus Alex. The aging north sider was on the stand three and a half days, telling the jury: "It didn't make sense to lie...I testified truthfully." Patrick explained he had to tell the truth otherwise, "They (prosecutors) are going to tear up the (plea) agreement and I'm going to spend the rest of my life in prison."

The plea agreement was for Patrick to serve a six year prison term but that was reduced to about four years. Whether Patrick ever went to a real prison is debatable.

Alex's lawyers had to defuse Patrick's testimony, so they portrayed the mob defector as a super deluxe con man who had falsely told his minions that he was working for Gus Alex.

That way, the defense argued, Patrick would get an extra share of the extortion proceeds, telling his crew that a large chunk of money had to go to Alex.

Patrick left the stand, as they say in show business, leaving them laughing. The aging mobster told the courtroom, "I can't remember everything. I'm not 20 years old."

The government's other major witness was James LaValley, an unindicted co-conspirator, who was cooperating with the Justice Department. LaValley, a burly 225 pounder, who had committed a rash of burglaries and beatings for the mob, gave the jurors a chilling inside look as to how an extortion scheme was carried out. LaValley, an enforcer for the Patrick crew, admitted he had never met Alex but knew of Alex through reputation. LaValley testified that Patrick told him he had to have Alex's okay before a victim was shaken down.

The jury listened intently to LaValley who described what it took to be an efficient enforcer. LaValley explained that it was harder to beat somebody up than kill him. Said LaValley, "If you want to give him a message, it will take some time."

Murder, La Valley pointed out is easier, "You can just walk up to somebody and kill him." LaValley implicated Patrick's crew member and defendant Nick Gio in two beatings and two arsons. To put frosting on the cake, LaValley told how he and Gio worked over a suburban restaurant operator who owned the Patrick crew some money. LaValley said he and Gio decked the victim and then began kicking him.

Prosecutor Gair: "You kicked a man on the ground?"

LaValley: "It ain't the girl scouts."

A number of businessmen who had run afoul of the Patrick crew took the stand to tell their tales of woe. One restaurant proprietor testified that he told a Patrick crew member that he was having trouble making $2,000 a month extortion payment. According to the witness, the Patrick crew member hinted he had better come up with the money, saying "They would find me dead in a freezer."

The defense took some pot shots at Patrick during closing arguments. Sam Adam let Patrick have it with both barrels, calling the turncoat mobster, "A piece of slime...the most evil snake you'll ever see...the evil incarnate."

Despite the verbal assault on Patrick's testimony and reputation the jury believed Patrick's contention that Alex was the overseer of the extortion ring. The ailing Alex was found guilty on October 1, 1992, of approving violent extortions. He was taken out of the courtroom in a wheelchair by U.S. Marshals and taken to the Metropolitan Correctional Center to await sentencing. A co-defendant Nick Gio, a member of Patrick's crew, was also found guilty. A third member of the Patrick operation, Mario Rainone, had pleaded guilty earlier. Prosecutor Gair and co-counsel, Mark Vogel, a career Strike Force prosecutor, were ecstatic about the verdict. It was a big win for the government.

For Alex it was the end of the line. Judge James Alesia imposed the maximum term on Alex when he sentenced the Mob's connection man to 15 years and eight months in prison. The Judge also ordered the 76 year old Alex to pay $823,000 in fines and restitution. Prosecutor Gair in calling for a substantial sentence called Alex, "The Gentlemen Gangster who spun his evil from his Gold Coast apartment, sending out legbreakers to do his bidding." Carl Walsh who had asked for mercy predicted that Alex would die in jail. Walsh's prediction was correct. In July, 1998, Alex died of a heart attack at the Federal Prison Center in Lexington, Kentucky. He was 82 years old.

Patrick hardly had time to catch his breath before he was testifying for the government once more, this time at a mob trial in San Diego, California. By now it had dawned on Patrick that he did not have immunity from prosecution when he testified at the Alex proceeding about being involved in six murders. There is no statue of limitations on murders so Patrick was in hot water. Patrick admitted the six slayings were either premeditated or done in a moment of passion when he was on the stand in Chicago. But in San Diego, Patrick changed his tune, claiming, under oath, that all of the six killings were in self-defense.

Federal prosecutors hit the ceiling when they learned what had happened on the west coast. They wanted to put the "kibosh" on Patrick's plea agreement and possibly try him for perjury. Perjury was the least of Lenny's troubles—the Cook County States Attorneys' office charged him with three of those murders.

But in the end, it really didn't matter. In November, 1996, a Judge found Patrick unfit to stand trial. Expert testimony said Lenny was suffering from dementia and could not assist in his own defense. So at the age of 83, Patrick was off the hook and placed in the witness protection program and was able to live out the remainder of his "golden years" outside of prison walls.

Patrick's epitaph could be summed up by Chris Gair who said, "He was one of the scariest people I ever met. There wasn't much to like about Lenny Patrick."

16

HAIL CAESAR

Al Tocco succeeded Al Pilotto in Chicago Heights.

He once supposedly left a half million dollars in a flower pot at an Athens apartment. No, he didn't forget the cash. He was forced to exit the apartment in such a hurry because he had been rousted by Greek police and was being expelled from the country.

That was Albert Caesar Tocco, the mob's south suburban rackets' boss in the 1980s. He fled the U.S. shortly before he was indicted by the federal government on racketeering and extortion charges. Tocco was a big fish when he was finally netted by the Justice Department, but he was a little fish for many years.

Tocco was born poor on August 9, 1929, in suburban Chicago Heights. He hailed from a section in the Heights known as Hungry Hill, where he knew poverty as a child. Tocco, who attended schools in Bloom Township, wasn't inclined for the academic life. He said at his trial that he had only a 7th grade education. But he made up for that with a share of street smarts and as a young bookmaker he attracted the attention of associates of Frank LaPorte, the crime syndicate overseer of the rackets in the south suburbs, Will County, and northwest Indiana.

Tocco was on his way as a crime syndicate soldier. Soon he moved up the ladder after serving his apprenticeship. When LaPorte left the scene, Tocco allied himself with Al Pilotto, the longtime mob boss in the south suburbs. Tocco was becoming a person to be reckoned with.

Tocco was never one to wait for the grass to grow. Gambling, the chop shop racket, juice loans, prostitution, extortion, and other illegal activities would keep most mobsters' noses to the grindstone. But, not Tocco. In addition to the above sources of income, he operated vending machines, ran a waste hauling business, and had his own restaurant. His waste hauling business was particularly lucrative. At one point he had a garbage disposal contract with the city of Chicago Heights. His middle name was Caesar and he ran the show to make sure that his troops rendered unto Caesar what was Caesar's.

Although he had his foot in the door in so many enterprises, he didn't like publicity. Once when a Channel Two News crew staked out his restaurant in order to get a tape of Tocco, the veteran Outfit boss donned a Groucho Marx style nose and glasses as he cooked on the grill by a front window. The move may have been counterproductive though. Because it was so humorous the tape was played many times by the station, much to the delight of the viewers and probably to the consternation of Tocco. On another occasion he dashed out of the Dirksen Federal Building with a jacket over his head to conceal his face. Once on the street he put on the after-burners as he ran up Wabash Avenue with a WBBM-TV news crew in hot pursuit.

Tocco had an insatiable appetite for money and power. Most mobsters would have been content to serve as an aide de camp to the then south suburban boss Pilotto. There is no question that Tocco coveted Pilotto's position as the area leader. Whether he had any role in arranging the failed assassination attempt on Pilotto at a golf course in 1981 is a subject of debate. He was never charged for any role in the Pilotto shooting but he certainly had a lot to gain with Pilotto's demise. The murder attempt became a moot point in 1982 when the aging Pilotto was convicted on federal charges in Miami, Florida. Pilotto went to prison for a long time and no longer ran the show.

With Pilotto out of the picture, Tocco became "numero uno" in the south region. Tocco though had been under federal scrutiny long before the Pilotto shooting. His activities as a gambling boss in southern Cook County, Will County, and northwest Indiana had piqued the interest of the IRS. In December, 1980, dozens of IRS agents swooped down on nine locations seizing large amounts of cash and hundreds of gambling records that were turned over to a grand jury which was investigating mob gambling in the south suburbs. Those 1980 raids laid the groundwork for an indictment on the Tocco gambling empire.

Three years later on August 17, 1983, the Justice Department fired a salvo at the Tocco organization. Tocco and eleven associates were indicted on charges that they operated an illegal bookmaking business from July, 1971, through 1981.The indictment alleged that the defendants accepted bets on football, basketball, and baseball, as well as wagers on horse races. Tocco was charged with failure to register as a bookmaker with the IRS, failing to pay the IRS an occupational tax, and gambling conspiracy.

The case looked like a slam dunk. The Strike Force prosecutors were certain that they had the goods on Tocco. However, it didn't work out that way. When the dust of battle cleared Tocco walked away a free man. The jury spent some 16 hours over a two day period before acquitting Tocco. The jury did convict seven other defendants, including two of Al's lieutenants, but those convictions were on relatively minor charges, misdemeanors, carrying sentences of one year in prison and a $1,000 fine.

Tocco's attorney Pat Tuite, a prominent criminal lawyer, admitted that Tocco placed bets for himself but Tuite told the jury that his client never accepted bets for others. Tuite scoffed at suggestions that Tocco was some kind of gambling kingpin. Apparently the jury agreed with Tuite.

The Strike Force was very upset at the outcome of the trial. Prosecutors thought they had a strong case. But instead of throwing in the towel the Feds felt a rematch with Tocco was in order, not on gambling charges, but something a lot more serious.

While federal agents were again investigating Tocco's empire, stories circulated that the south suburban crime boss was connected to a Mexican drug smuggling network. A Customs Department intelligence report that I'd received alleged "that Tocco provides the financial base and exercises control over a majority of all narcotic related activities engaged in by lower echelon figures." The analysis also contended "that Tocco's organization is a regular supplier for two major street gangs in Chicago (the El Rukns and the Black Disciples Nation)."

If that was true, it would fly in the face of the Outfit's policies in the 1980s, that drug activity was strictly a no no. Then in the summer of 1989, the Brownsville, Texas, *Herald* reported a possible link between the Tocco organization and a Mexican drug smuggling gang based in Matamoros, Mexico. The drug ring was believed responsible for smuggling tons of cocaine and marijuana into the U.S. Lawyer Tuite, when contacted by the media, called the newspaper report "absolute nonsense."

In justice to Tocco the Strike Force never contended, at least publicly, that Tocco was involved in narcotics trafficking. Uncle Sam wasn't concerned with Tocco's alleged involvement in drugs (some agents didn't believe he was connected to illegal drugs). They were after him for bigger things. It was soon evident that the Feds were going for a full court press on the beleaguered mob boss.

In March, 1988, FBI agents raided Tocco's ranch style home in Bloom Township, seizing about 30 cartons of records regarding his former waste hauling business. At about the same time investigators were talking to people in auto junkyards and night clubs that were reportedly paying a street tax to the Tocco organization.

It was obvious that an indictment was soon forthcoming, and in October, 1988, the other shoe fell. Tocco and one of his lieutenants, Clarence Crockett, also known as Ed Woods, were indicted on racketeering and extortion charges. The government charged that the two men were practicing the old protection racket in extorting money from auto salvage yards and houses of prostitution.

Announcing the indictment U.S. Attorney Anton Valukas told reporters that "in the past persons who engaged in this activity (shakedowns and racketeering) felt they were immune from prosecution because of their ability to intimidate witnesses...our intent is to end this immunity."

Court buffs eagerly looked forward to the upcoming trial which they felt would be a "Jim Dandy." But before a trial date could be fixed Tocco disappeared, allegedly with several hundred thousand dollars in cash on him. Tocco cleared out several bank accounts in the Chicago area to tide him over while he became a fugitive. The $64,000 question was where did Tocco go?

Well, Tocco was caught because he wanted to see his seven year old son again. The FBI located Tocco by following the youngster who led them to his father. The boy and an unidentified adult (reportedly his mother) flew out of O'Hare Field on the day after Christmas. The flight took young Tocco to

Athens, Greece, where he met his Dad. It seemed the elder Tocco had been in Greece for some time before the indictment was returned. He smelled a rat and decided to vamoose.

While Tocco and his boy were being surveilled in Athens, the FBI put pressure on the Greek government to have the south suburban rackets' boss expelled. It seemed Tocco had not disclosed his criminal background when he entered the country. He also had consorted with a Greek mobster which didn't do him any good with the Greek authorities. So the bottom line was that Tocco was expelled and an international manhunt was over.

Chicago FBI agent John Bonino said Tocco was not a happy camper when he arrived at the terminal in Athens in the custody of Greek police. He was kicking and screaming. He didn't want to get on that plane. But board he did. The mob boss didn't realize that as the plane headed for Rome on the first leg of the trip to Chicago that some of his seatmates were FBI agents from the Chicago office. He told fellow pas-

Al Tocco—When he was older. Fled to Greece.

senger Neal O'Malley, an undercover FBI agent, that he was rousted so fast out of his apartment that he didn't have any money on him. He complained to O'Malley that he had left a half million dollars hidden in a flower pot. If Tocco had stashed that amount of money in the flower pot it wasn't found by Greek police when they searched the apartment. At least that's what Greek authorities said.

Tocco complained about other alleged injustices on the Rome flight not realizing the identity of O'Malley. Tocco, according to accounts, got so angry on the plane that he tried to knock out a window.

When the flight de-planed in Rome the agents revealed their identity, causing Tocco to blurt out, "The trickster has been tricked."

It was during the layover in Rome that the 59 year old Tocco became more friendly, boasting of his physical prowess. According to agent O'Malley, Tocco challenged an Italian policeman, who was obviously a weight lifter, to a one arm push up contest. The push up contest between Tocco and the Italian cop never came off but Tocco related to his captors that he kept in shape while in prison by doing one arm push ups. O'Malley said Tocco enjoyed repartee telling the agent, "I like to bust balls."

At a pre-trial hearing agent Bonino testified that he sat with the mob boss on the long flight from Rome to Chicago. When the flight neared New York Tocco asked the agent if the government would take a guilty plea in return for a ten year sentence. But in such a deal, Tocco would have had to cooperate with the Justice Department in cases involving mob activities. Apparently that was no dice for Tocco. At the same hearing Tocco took the stand and indicated he was never interested in such a deal. Said Tocco, "I got spots on me (like a leopard) and they don't rub off. I'm not a stool pigeon."

The trial itself did not begin until November of 1989, with interest in the case growing. But before jury selection could begin Judge James Holderman granted a government motion that the identities of the jurors would not be revealed. Holderman made his ruling after prosecutors contended that unless the jurors' identities were protected, there was likelihood that jurors would be apprehensive about their safety and that of their families. Such a procedure is rare and courtroom observers said in 1989 that this was the first time that a jury was selected by number, not name in a case at the Dirksen Federal Building.

When the trial got into high gear it lived up to its advance billing. Like the court buffs predicted it was "juicy." Jurors heard testimony about gangland murders, shakedowns of taverns, brothels, chop shops, and payoffs to police.

Prosecutors said one strip club, the Show Club, a haven for visiting "butter and egg men," paid off Tocco over a three and a half year period. The government said an aging madam, Valerie Walker, paid the Tocco crew a street tax so she could continue to operate. Walker testified she paid Tocco bagman Clarence Crockett $400 a month because she feared for her life and that of her employees.

Also paying off the Tocco faction, according to prosecutors, were five suburban auto parts yards, known in the trade as chop shops, because they dealt in parts from stolen cars. The chop shop operators couldn't complain to the authorities since their operations were also illegal.

The FBI had contended that Tocco was linked to nine gangland murders. He was never charged with murder, but sleuths said he had ordered the hits or was involved one way or another in the slayings.

Some of the most damaging testimony came when Robert Hardin, a one time associate of the defendant took the stand. Judge Holderman asked courtroom artists to distort Hardin's feature to protect him from possible gangland retribution. The 44 year old Hardin was in the witness protection program and had been relocated and given a new identity.

Hardin himself was no saint. He admitted, under oath, that he personally killed three people, was involved in countless burglaries and car thefts. He testified under a grant of immunity and was getting a break in a pending drug case against him. According to Hardin, Tocco ordered four murders, including the slayings of mob hit man William Dauber and his wife Charlotte, who were gunned down in July, 1980. The Justice Department believed Dauber was slain because fellow mobsters had found out that Dauber had become a government informant. Dauber's wife happened to be in the wrong place at the wrong time.

Hardin said the 1975 murder of Milwaukee crime syndicate figure August Maniaci was done at Tocco's request. Maniaci had supposedly owed Tocco a lot of money and had been slow in repaying it. And Hardin told the jury that the murder of south suburban vending company operator Dino Valente was ordered because the South Holland man was muscling in on Tocco's turf.

But the prosecution's star witness was not a reformed hit man but the estranged wife of Tocco. Forty year old Betty Tocco, a one time swimsuit and lingerie model, took the witness strand to be the first outfit leader's wife, at least in recent memory, to testify against her husband. Betty told the packed court room about life as a mob queen, describing Al's syndicate affiliations and the couple's affluent lifestyle.

Her testimony so angered Tocco that he shouted in court, "She's a liar. She'll always be a liar." Al was so enraged that he asked to be excused and was placed in a holding cell adjacent to the courtroom. Tocco's lawyers Pat Tuite and James Shellow hammered away at Betty's credibility contending she was lying in an effort to send her husband to prison. That way, they explained, Betty could receive a large share of Al's estate.

But the biggest bombshell from Betty came later in a sentencing memorandum in which she claimed she picked Al up one June night in a northwest Indiana farm field. Tocco, according to Betty, needed a ride home. Al, as Betty explained, was all shook up saying he had just buried the Spilotro brothers. Las Vegas mob boss Tony Spilotro and his younger brother Michael were slain in June, 1986, and their bodies were buried in a corn field near Morocco, Indiana.

Rosalind Rossi, a *Chicago Sun Times* federal building reporter, obtained an exclusive interview with Betty after the trial. It was then that Mrs. Tocco elaborated on the burial story. Rossi reported that Mrs. Tocco told her that it was Father's Day and her husband's mother and sister were coming over. Rossi quoted Mrs. Tocco as saying, "What was I supposed to say? Albert just buried the Spilotros last night, so we can't barbecue today."

In a court document federal authorities wrote that Tocco, upon hearing that the gravesite was discovered, became concerned that Mob boss Joe Ferriola would have him killed because of incompetence. However, Tocco was not slain. According to court documents Ferriola had forgiven him.

The court buffs, who sat through the entire proceedings and heard from 48 government witnesses, predicted that Tocco and Crockett would be convicted. In the Court Watchers newsletter of December 5, 1989, the shadow jury, as the buffs called themselves, said it would be a slam dunk for the prosecution. There were no dissenters among the buffs as to the outcome of the case.

It took the jury of seven men and five women about eight hours to reach its verdict. Tocco showed no emotion when the panel found him guilty of extorting money from chop shops, houses of prostitution, and other illegal enterprises. Tocco was also convicted of arranging the murders of mob hit man William Dauber and his wife Charlotte. Co-defendant Crockett, the Tocco bag man, also bit the dust. Clarence was convicted of racketeering, extortion, and income tax violations.

The buffs in their newsletter summed up the prosecution and defense teams this way: Larry "The Harvard Hotshot" Rosenthal and Dean "Lefty" Polales beat two of America's premier lawyers, James Shallow of Milwaukee and Patrick Tuite." But the buffs said "Quick With the Quip" Tuite, as they called him, did a good job in a losing cause.

After the verdicts were read prosecutor Rosenthal told Judge James Holderman that Tocco had threatened him in a court hallway on November 28th. According to Rosenthal, Tocco said, "I'm going to get you. I'm going to get the FBI agents." Tocco, though angrily denied making such a comment. He said to Holderman, "You know he is lying." Tocco and Crockett were then hustled out of the courtroom and taken to the Metropolitan Correctional Center to await sentencing.

On May 14, 1990 Tocco had the dubious honor of receiving the stiffest sentence ever handed down to a Chicago mob leader. Judge Holderman gave Tocco a virtual death sentence, 200 years in a federal prison. Tocco went down with guns blazing. Addressing the court he said, "I'm no crime boss....I never gave no orders for no murders."

Earlier Holderman had sentenced Crockett, described by some mob watchers as a member of the Hillbilly Mafia, to a 20 year prison term.

Tocco was an inmate at several prisons before his death. For a time he was at Marion, then the toughest federal pen. It was there we wrote Tocco to see if he was interested in giving his side of the story through an interview. He never replied.

Al kept a tight rein on his troops and was widely feared by his subordinates. FBI agent Wayne Zydron, who kept track of Tocco in the south suburbs, said he was not a man to be trifled with. Zydron said, "Lots of people were scared shitless of him in the Heights."

Another FBI agent, Bob Pecoraro was quoted as saying "Just the way he was looking at you, just the way he talked to you was scary."

Clarence Crockett—member of the Hillbilly Mafia.

Tocco never saw the light of day after his sentencing. He died after suffering a stroke on September 21, 2005 in the federal prison at Terre Haute, Indiana. He was 76 years old.

His partner in crime Clarence Crockett followed him in death six months later. Crockett was 68 years old when he died of natural causes at his home in Chicago Heights. He had been released from prison in 2001.

When Tocco went to prison an aging suburban Orland Park man, Dominic "Tootsie" Palermo, filled in as boss. At least that's what federal authorities said. But Palermo's reign was brief. Soon after Palermo settled in as Tocco's successor, he and five members of his crime family were indicted for extorting money from illegal gambling operators. Palermo, by the way, was one of the men who allegedly helped bury the Spilotro brothers.

"Tootsie" and his cohorts were convicted in 1991 and were sent to prison the following year. Palermo got a stiff sentence from Federal Judge James Moody in Hammond. Palermo's attorney Kevin Milner had called government allegations against his client "hogwash." Judge Moody, though, was not swayed, handing Palermo a 32 year sentence. Afterwards Milner told reporters that the jail term amounted to a death sentence for Palermo.

Milner was right. In April, 2005, Palermo died at the federal prison hospital in Rochester, Minnesota. He was 88. The Tocco era was over.

17

THE PORN KING

Reuben Sturman—Cleveland man known as The Porn King.

He called himself the Porn King, and I don't think there were any serious challengers to that dubious title. That was Reuben Sturman who was once labeled the top distributor of hard core pornography in the country. *Time* magazine even called Sturman, "The Bill Gates of porn."

Sturman's film or video tapes were never nominated for an Oscar but they made money. The titles of some of those money makers: "Dr. Bizzaro," "Between the Cheeks," "The Nurse Will See You Now," and "You Said A Mouthful." They were not classics of the silver screen. Assuming most of our readers never saw these films we'll enlighten you as to what they were about.

Some dealt with women having sexual relations with horses, pigs and other animals, while others were even more gross, featuring scenes of humans eating excrement, while still others had scenes of sado-masochism. We could go into other details, but I think the reader gets the idea about the contents.

By the mid 1930s Sturman had become a national figure and was one of the first entrepreneurs to realize the significance of videotape. He dubbed his films onto videotape, distributed hard-core porn to outlets all over the country, and then expanded his operation to outlets in England, the Netherlands, and Germany.

Sturman was successful in his field but it wasn't handed to him on a silver platter. He wasn't born with a silver spoon in his mouth. He came from modest circumstances. Reuben Sturman was born in Cleveland in 1924. After a stint in the Army Air Force during World War II, he returned to the Forest City and with the aid of the G.I. bill attended Western Reserve University. But let Sturman tell in his own words how he got started in the porn business.

We interviewed Sturman at the Metropolitan Correctional Center in downtown Chicago where he was being held while awaiting trial on extortion charges. It was one of many legal tussles he had with the Justice Department since he became successful in the porn business. This is what Sturman said about his early days in Cleveland.

"I started in 1951, selling comic books out of the back of my car. I built that up, until five or six years later, I was called the comic book king of America. And then we got into the adult material sometime in the early 1960s. And about the same time, the movie *Deep Throat* came along and that sort of became, sort of a cult thing, and it became very popular."

Drummond interview with Sturman in the Federal lock-up.

So Sturman, realizing there was much more money in porn than in comic books, began publishing sex books and selling them in retail stores that he owned. He also introduced the peep booth in his stores. Peep shows had been around since day one. But Sturman set up a peep booth where patrons could watch their favorite porn flick in private behind a locked door. Never one not to get in on the ground floor, Sturman both manufactured peep booths and serviced them. If rival entrepreneurs wanted peep booths for their stores, Sturman accommodated them, on the house, in other words free of charge. The fly in the ointment was that Sturman in turn received half of the receipts.

It wasn't long before Sturman's activities aroused the interest of the Justice Department. In 1964 federal agents raided a warehouse in Cleveland and confiscated close to 600 copies of a paperback called, *Sex Life Of A Cop*. The 1964 raid triggered a war between Uncle Sam and Sturman that didn't end until the Clevelander died.

A grand jury indicted Sturman on federal obscenity charges. Sturman didn't take it lying down. He sued J. Edgar Hoover and the obscenity charges were dropped. The government has a long memory; Sturman had thrown down the gauntlet, and it was something Washington didn't forget.

Sturman skated on two other obscenity charges in 1976 and 1980. He became the poster boy in the sex industry because as people in the industry put it, he stood up to the Washington bureaucrats and won. The Justice department though had just begun to fight.

Sturman had moved part of his empire to Las Vegas. There his adult book store in the gambling mecca served as a major distribution center for adult books, magazines, videotapes, and other sexually explicit materials. Sturman was tops in his field and was beginning to be a burr in the side of law enforcement. His activities had attracted the attention of the government brass. In one of his clashes with the federal government, Washington felt that Sturman was so big that an indictment against him was announced by U.S. Attorney General Edwin Meese.

Observers believed for some time that Sturman had been paying off the Mafia and paid street taxes to the Gambino crime family. In our jail house interview he claimed he was his own boss and denied being in cahoots with the crime syndicate. Several knowledgeable sources I talked to found that very hard to believe. They felt it would have been difficult for Sturman to operate without having any mob ties.

In Chicago the porn industry has been plagued with pay offs, beatings, bombings, and even murder. Sturman himself was involved with some tough characters in Chicago, as we shall see.

At one point when adult book stores were found all over Chicago, a special city council sub-committee was assigned to investigate pornography. That was in 1977 when there were 59 adult book stores thriving in the city. The committee found that 35 of the porno shops were suspected of having ties to organized crime. The remainder, if they were successful at all, undoubtedly had to pay a street tax or protection money to the Outfit if they wanted to stay in business.

Many of those who tried to remain independent (or free of mob control) had "visitors." A Chicago woman who was considered a local mogul in the porn distribution field reportedly was targeted for assassination by remote control bomb. The woman had not been paying tribute to the syndicate.

In another incident two men were arrested after they were seen fleeing from a bookstore they had trashed. The two men had mob ties. But then things got more ugly. Beatings and threats were one thing, but murder was another.

In September, 1976, the owner or co-owner of seven porno movie houses was shot seven times in broad daylight in Chicago's Old Town area. The victim was 33 year old Paul Gonsky, a 250 pound resident of north suburban Deerfield. Gonsky apparently felt he had his share of enemies, since he carried a 38 caliber revolver. Unfortunately for Gonsky he didn't have a chance to use the weapon. He was gunned down in a parking lot not far from the Bijou Theater where he had his office. Although Gonsky's gun was recovered, the murder weapon, believed to have been a 22 caliber semi-automatic with a silencer, was never found.

A year and a half before the shooting, Gonsky's car, a Porsche, was blown up as it sat in Gonsky's driveway in Deerfield. The bombing was obviously a message that Gonsky didn't heed. In attempting to determine a motive, there were several theories that investigators explored.

1. The mob was muscling Gonsky and they wanted to take over his theater empire. 2. A business rival who was involved in a legal dispute with Gonsky might have wanted to get rid of the Deerfield man permanently. 3. Or was the fact that Gonsky's projectionists were non-union a factor? That seems very unlikely. The projectionists union had been involved in

some strong arm tactics with theater owners but murder was a different story. Despite an intensive investigation the case remains unsolved more than 30 years after Gonsky was slain.

Then in 1985, nine years after Gonsky's murder, Patrick "Patsy" Ricciardi's body was found in the trunk of a car. Ricciardi, who was 59, had been shot in the back and head. His trouser pockets had been turned inside out and as much as $1,000 was missing. Some detectives speculated that the trouser gimmick indicated that Ricciardi owed money.

Ricciardi was the owner of the Admiral Theater, the top showplace for porno films in Chicago. At one time the Admiral was open seven days a week from nine in the morning until midnight, featuring a steady diet of pornographic movies. And Ricciardi once had clout. He was the cousin of the late Felix "Milwaukee Phil" Alderisio, a mob enforcer who died in 1971. Prior to Ricciardi's involvement in the adult movie business, he was identified by authorities as a crime syndicate loan shark.

"Patsy" had told a daughter that he was meeting an unidentified person on the north side. That was on a Wednesday. His family reported him missing on Thursday and on Friday his body was discovered in a stolen Oldsmobile, found abandoned, not too far from where Ricciardi was to have met someone. Ricciardi's murder, like Gonsky, remains unsolved. Although police have a prime suspect, he has never been charged.

The murders of Gonsky and Ricciardi made a strong impression on the few adult book store owners who had no connection to the syndicate. It was pay up or else.

But one operator, William "Red" Wemette, was fed up and was tired of eating humble pie. Wemette owned a store on north Wells Street and he let the FBI place a hidden video recording device in his apartment. When mob collectors came calling to get their street tax, their conversations as well as their "mugs" were recorded for posterity.

The FBI sting netted a pretty big fish, Frank "The German" Schweihs, a mob enforcer of some note. Schweihs was convicted of shaking down Wemette and "The German" was sentenced to 10 years in a federal prison. A confederate of Schweihs, who used to pinch hit for the veteran mobster, also received a prison term for his role in the shakedown scheme.

About the same time that Schweihs was under scrutiny, Michael "The Fireplug" Glitta succumbed to a heart attack. Authorities said that the 68 year old Glitta was the local overseer of the mob's pornography operations in Chicago. Only a year before his death, Glitta's younger brother Marco was sentenced to eight years in prison for purchasing two remote control bombs. Prosecutors surmised that the younger Glitta ordered the bombs to either kill or send a message to Paula Lawrence by blowing up a building where Paula did business. Lawrence, an associate of Sturman, was a business rival who distributed sexually explicit movies and magazines to other cities.

Federal Judge Milton Shadur turned a deaf ear to Glitta's plea for leniency. Glitta's story also drew guffaws from court buffs, on hand for the sentencing. Marco Glitta claimed he was just kidding when he told two government informants that he wanted the bombs to send a message. No, Marco Glitta contended, he wanted only to tinker with the bombs, not to use them in any destructive way. Although Judge Shadur didn't buy Glitta's story, prison officials let him out long enough to attend his brother Michael's funeral.

Meanwhile, the Justice Department was zeroing in on Sturman during this period. In 1987 Sturman was convicted in Cleveland of conspiracy to defraud, and of not paying $3,000,000 in federal income tax. By now the King of Porn had become a national figure and his trial received heavy media coverage. Playing the clown, Sturman would enter and leave the courthouse in a bizarre mask with coke bottle glasses, a huge phony nose, and a Hitler-like mustache.

Although Sturman enjoyed putting on a show as he entered and left the Cleveland courthouse, he was not amused when Stephen H. Jigger, an attorney with the Justice Department's Organized Crime Strike Force, said Reuben was consumed by unadulterated greed. Jigger went on to say that literally every tax fraud scheme known to man was utilized by Rueben Sturman.

A federal judge apparently agreed with the government's argument and sentenced Sturman to 10 years in prison and fined him $2,460,000 for tax evasion. Sturman's attorney had argued that tax-related crimes usually result in smaller sentences. But that argument did not hold water in this case. Sturman, though was allowed to remain free on bond while he appealed the verdict and sentence.

Several years later in an interview, an angry Sturman told us that the government had a vendetta against him because he had beaten them on a number of occasions on obscenity charges. However, that win streak over the Justice department on obscenity allegations ended in 1992 when he pleaded guilty to racketeering and shipping obscene materials across state lines. He got a four year jail hitch on that one. But his biggest headache was yet to come.

The way federal authorities tell it, Sturman was behind a plot to bomb eight adult book stores in Chicago. Sturman, investigators say, didn't hire the bombers; he let a middleman do that. Members of a California motorcycle gang were hired to send a message to the book store owner so that he would resume payoffs. Apparently the owner was objecting to the extortion. It was like the old protection racket but the plot went awry when one of the bombs (the gang was using pipe bombs) went off prematurely and killed one of the would-be bombers.

The victim was identified as 28 year old Donald Mares of California who was riding in the front seat of a rental car driven by another biker. The bomb went off, ATF agents speculated, while Mares was fidgeting with a remote control device.

Aftermath of a car bombing scene. WBBM-TV photo.

Mares staggered out of the car and then collapsed to the pavement. The mishap occurred right in the heart of the Rush Street area night club district. The driver of the car fled the scene even though his hair and clothing had been scorched.

It wasn't long before federal authorities nabbed one of the bombing crew. He was 32 year old Jay Brissette, who admitted building and testing bombs in the California desert. Brissette also conceded that he and three other men had flown into Chicago for the purpose of bombing book stores. Brissette named his biker colleagues, who also threw in the towel.

Brissette said he and a companion had been promised $60,000 to do their work. Although he didn't know who was behind the plot, he apparently fingered Herbert "Mickey" Feinberg, AKA "Mickey Fein," as the man who paid him. Brissette, a flooring contractor by trade, and his biker pals all went to jail. Brissette, even though he cooperated, got a nine year stretch and was fined $6,800. The fine was for the rental car that was blown up in the pipe bomb accident that killed one of the bikers.

Sturman at this point was in jail after his appeal was denied, and then he vanished. That's right Sturman escaped from a minimum security institution in California. On December 7, 1992, while he was under investigation for the Chicago bomb plot, he took a powder. Authorities assumed he had fled the country and was gone for good. But that wasn't the case. Some eight weeks after his prison break Sturman was apprehended in a Florida apartment near Orlando. Sturman was later taken to Chicago where he was held at the Metropolitan Correctional Center in downtown Chicago to await trial on extortion charges.

It was there in August of 1993 that he explained to me why he escaped from prison. "Rumor was I was going to Colorado and my family couldn't visit me there. On impulse I walked away and it wasn't too bright." Sturman was concerned that he was going to be sent to the maximum security institution at Florence, Colorado, which was no country club.

While Sturman was at the MCC, the government was preparing its case against the man it described as the "Godfather" of pornographic peep shows. And the Justice Department had the goods. Prosecutors put a number of bookstore owners from Chicago, Cleveland, and Phoenix on the stand. They told of paying kickbacks of $60,000 to $100,000 every four to six weeks. The witnesses told the jury that when they squawked about such hefty payments Sturman began threatening them and then resorted to violence.

Before the trial, Sturman told us that he felt the government had no case, as far as extortion was concerned. He argued that he couldn't be guilty of extortion because he owned the businesses that were making payments. Sturman said, "I own the businesses that I'm supposedly extorting from. I'm extorting from my own businesses—that's part of our defense."

The six man-six women jury didn't go along with Sturman's hypothesis. After two days of deliberation, the jury found Sturman guilty of conspiring to extort money from adult bookstores in three states. However, Sturman was found not guilty in the attempted bombing. Court room observers believed that the jurors apparently felt that the bikers, who were hired by a Sturman associate, decided to escalate the violence on their own.

Sturman's confederate fared no better than his pal. In a separate trial a jury deliberated less than two hours before finding Herbert Feinberg guilty of hiring four men to damage and bomb several bookstores. The judge threw the book at the 63 year old Los Angeles resident. Senior U.S. Judge Warren Urbom sentenced Feinberg to 40 years in prison—30 years for the bombing and 10 years for extortion. At his age the prison term amounted to a death sentence for Feinberg. And indeed it was, as Feinberg who had a heart condition died in prison at the age of 64.

Sturman didn't fare much better. Judge Paul Plunkett sentenced the 70 year old to 19 years in prison. As was the case with Feinberg it was a death sentence, since Sturman also had to serve part of a ten year term on a tax conviction he had received in Cleveland. He was sent to a federal prison in Kentucky, defiant as ever. To the end Sturman claimed he was the victim of a government vendetta and continued to deny he was associated with the Gambino crime family or any other crime syndicate group. Several years later he died from a stroke in that Kentucky prison at the age of 73.

The pornography business has changed since an FBI agent called Sturman the biggest porn distributor in the world. Nowadays people watch hard core pornography in their homes on cable TV, video, or VCRs. And with hand held video cameras anyone can shoot porn in their home with friends and spouses if they chose.

As one porn executive explained, "Why watch the stuff at a theater or bookstore when you can see the same stuff in the privacy of your living room?"

18

THE NOVICE HIT MAN

I've heard of mob hits in cars, in alleys, in restaurants, on sidewalks, in garages, outside of hotels, and even in a victim's home. Remember Sam Giancana? But never can I recall of an outfit "gunsel" practicing his wares on a Chicago area golf course.

Al Pilotto—south suburban rackets' boss.

Yet it happened on July 25, 1981, at the Lincolnshire Country Club in Crete, a suburb south of Chicago. The intended victim was Al Pilotto, a south suburban rackets' boss and Laborer's Union official. Pilotto was shot five times by the gunman but survived to eventually testify at a trial against the two men who conspired to murder him.

Pilotto, who was 71 at the time of the shooting, was no Casper Milquetoast type. According to federal authorities, he was the boss of the mob's south group based in Chicago Heights. Pilotto was described by FBI agents as one of five street bosses under the tutelage of Joey "The Doves" Aiuppa, the operating director of the Chicago mob.

James York, an FBI agent from Chicago, said Pilotto ran the far south side "overseeing gambling, extortion, prostitution, and collections from chop shop gangs that profited by stealing vehicles and then selling the parts."

In June, 1981, one month before Pilotto was shot, the Chicago Heights man was one of 16 persons indicted by a federal grand jury in Miami on racketeering charges. The defendants, including Chicago Outfit boss Tony Accardo, were charged in connection with a kickback scheme that prosecutors said milked $2,000,000 from the Laborers Union benefits fund. I remember when the indictment came down. I told Chicago Strike force members that their news release had listed Pilotto's age as 71 which obviously was incorrect. It turned out that Pilotto indeed was 71. Well, he was the youngest 71 year old that I had ever seen. Pilotto looked the picture of health.

The government claimed that organized crime elements wanted Pilotto killed to keep him from testifying in the upcoming racketeering case in which one of his co-defendants was Accardo. Mob higherups feared that Pilotto was getting senile and that he would turn informant and begin spilling names rather than risk going to trial where he might be convicted and sent to jail. But Pilotto never turned what underworld figures would call a "rat." As we will find out later, Pilotto never testified in the trial which occurred in the spring of 1982.

Now on that warm July morning back in 1981, Pilotto and his foursome had just arrived at the 8th tee when the shooting occurred. Pilotto was playing with Sam Guzzino, Rudy

Al Pilotto—at the Federal Courthouse in Chicago after 1981 indictment. WBBM-TV photo.

Bamonti, and Nick Fushi. We have no idea what the handicaps were of the four, but they were avid golfers. Pilotto had just teed off and was putting his driver back into the golf cart when a man suddenly came out of the woods and began shooting.

As Pilotto recounted later the assailant first shot him in the arm and then kept shooting as he walked toward him. The south side mob boss, who was shot five times, said the gunman got to within a foot of him and then ran away. The would-be "torpedo" had blasted Pilotto with a .357 revolver. Al was lucky to escape with his life. No shots were fired at Pilotto's golfing companions.

We don't know if Pilotto's partners finished their round after the mob chieftain was shot. It would not be too far fetched, if the men were avid golfers. I recall an AP story in the 1990s where a golfer was stricken with a fatal heat attack on a green at a course in Florida. The foursome on the tee got impatient and began firing their tee shots at the green on the par 3 hole. The stricken golfer's partners objected but that didn't deter the other foursome who putted out on the hole before the paramedics arrived.

Pilotto had been shot in the leg, arm, and shoulder and was rushed to St. James Hospital in Chicago Heights where he underwent surgery. Pilotto's brother Henry was the police chief of Chicago Heights, and although Al was not assigned a police guard, some police officers and a number of the wounded man's friends patrolled inside and outside the building.

Al was questioned by Crete police officers when he was well enough to talk the next day. According to them, Pilotto would only say no when asked if he knew who shot him. But Pilotto did say that his assailant was a tall, thin, white man who wore a mask. It turned out that the shooter was tall, thin, and white.

When it became obvious that Pilotto was going to survive the assassination attempt, the shooter fled after he had heard rumors that Al had ordered him killed. Then in October, three months after the attempt on Pilotto's life, one of Al's golfing partners, Sam Guzzino, was found dead in a ditch near Beecher, Illinois. The 51 year old Guzzino had been shot in the head and his throat had been cut. Authorities theorized that Pilotto had ordered the hit on Guzzino because he believed that Guzzino had orchestrated his assassination. There was no doubt, investigators felt, that Sam Guzzino was a major conspirator in the plot against Pilotto. The death of Sam Guzzino prompted Sam's younger brother, Richard, one of the conspirators, to go into hiding,

The shooter, identified as 26 year old Daniel Bounds, was on the lam for a time, traveling to Atlanta, Texas, and Arkansas before throwing in the towel and surrendering to authorities. Bounds, by the way, was the former son-in-law of the same Sam Guzzino whose body was found in a ditch.

Bounds, fearing that he was doomed and would soon be a victim of gangland retribution, turned himself in to Bill Lambie of the Chicago Crime Commission who in turn handed Bounds over to the FBI.

Bounds laid his cards on the table when he told the agents, "It's either get protection from you or risk being killed. I know they are after me."

Bounds had few options but to begin cooperating. Shortly after surrendering to the FBI the would-be hit man was put to work by agents who had him call his fellow conspirator Richard Guzzino. The conversations were taped. The two talked about life on the run, the fear of being killed by disciples of Pilotto, and financial woes, particularly those of Bounds.

Bounds was paranoid about being slain, telling Guzzino, "My name is at the top of the list. I'm sure the list is no invitation to a ball game. It's a hit list and I know there are two contracts out on me."

Guzzino scoffed at Bounds' fears and his concern about reprisals from the mob. In a December 1, 1981, conversation Guzzino warns Bounds that he is on his own.

Bounds: "All right I'll just lay low and do the best I can."

Guzzino: "Just remember what I told you, that's just lay low and stay out of the fuckin' town."

In a December 23, 1981, conversation Guzzino moans about his own financial situation and says he can't take care of Bounds.

Guzzino: "I ain't ever had much partner. My brother had everything I got and I didn't wind up with shit. You want to talk about the short end of the stick. I owe you nothing. I have nothing to give you." Guzzino was cagey in his conversations, not admitting any role in the shooting.

But Bounds, giving his version of the scenario, told the FBI that he was recruited by his former father-in-law Sam Guzzino. For a hit man Bounds came cheap. Bounds said he was offered $2,000 for the job plus a monthly stipend and a chance to work at one of the firms Sam Guzzino owned. Sam Guzzino operated a taxi service, a sausage factory, and the Vagabond Lounge, a bar in Chicago Heights that featured exotic dancing.

But there was a bonus in the proposition, too. Guzzino offered his former son-in-law permission to visit his young daughter (Sam Guzzino's granddaughter) from his estranged wife, Peri Guzzino. So the Chicago Heights cab driver took the contract.

Initially Bounds was not told who the victim was. Sam explained the hit was to be accomplished soon but he declined to identify the target because as Guzzino explained, "The less you know about it, the better you are."

However, two days before the shooting Sam Guzzino showed Bounds a videotape of a birthday party that Pilotto had attended. Bounds recalled that Guzzino stopped the videotape and pointed at Pilotto, "This is the guy I want killed." When Bounds realized that the intended victim was a mobster, Guzzino reportedly replied, "Don't worry about it. It's been blessed. " Bounds interpreted that to mean that the hit was sanctioned by higher-ups.

The next day Bounds met with Sam Guzzino and his younger brother, Richard Guzzino at Sam's cab company. Richard Guzzino expressed confidence in Bounds, adding that he himself was too fat to handle it, otherwise he would have loved to do it. Richard weighed well over 300 pounds

The following day Sam Guzzino and Bounds drove to a residence where there was a sign "bike for sale." Guzzino gave Bounds 20 dollars to buy the bike which was to be the getaway vehicle. But when Bounds tried the bike the gears and chain kept slipping, and the twosome gave up on the idea of using a bike in the assassination.

Several years later when the conspiracy case was up for appeal, one federal judge noted, "Were this attempted murder case not so serious, a recitation of some of the facts might suggest a Marx Brothers skit instead of a relationship to organized crime."

The next step for the crew was to improve Bounds' marksmanship. The third member of the conspiracy, Robert Ciarrocchi, entered the scene. Ciarrocchi, Sam Guzzino, and Bounds drove to as dump in Will County so that the novice hit man could improve his marksmanship. There, according to Bounds, Ciarrocchi handed him a .357 Magnum and a .45 caliber pistol. The target was a keep out sign at the dump. Ciarrocchi praised Bounds for emptying both guns into the sign. The would-be killer has passed his first test.

Bounds was then driven to a K-Mart where Sam Guzzino bought a green jump suit, a baseball cap, and a knapsack. Sam also lent Bounds his boots, even though they were much too big for the would-be killer. The gear was needed to camouflage Bounds so he could blend in with the bushes.

The next day Friday, July 24, 1981, the gang staged a dress rehearsal. Bounds hid in the bushes near the 8th tee. At the appointed time Sam Guzzino rode up in a golf cart accompanied by Ciarrocchi. Sam got out of the car and in a loud voice said, "Are you there?" Bounds responded and then Sam tried to find him and finally remarked. "That's great, that's beautiful." Bounds continued the dress rehearsal by running to the rendezvous point so that he could be timed.

Then it was showtime, Saturday July 25th. Bounds shaved off his moustache and made a nylon stocking mask which he would put on for the shooting. At 2:25 a.m., before the crack of dawn, Bounds got up to carry out his grisly assignment. Bounds was picked up by Ciarrocchi who drove him to his apartment where Ciarrocchi loaded two pistols and wiped the guns and ammunition free of fingerprints. He also provided Bounds with a pair of gloves, which like the boots, were too big for Bounds.

Sam Guzzino arrived at Ciarrocchi's apartment to give Bounds a pep talk. Guzzino said "everything is go" and that the foursome was scheduled to tee off at six a.m. According to Bounds, Sam Guzzino told him to walk up to Pilotto and put the "gun to his head and shoot. That's the Italian way. You've got to shoot him in the head."

By the time the foursome rode up to the 8th tee, Bounds was lying in wait in the bushes. Bounds heard Guzzino say, "Go ahead and shoot." The assailant assumed Sam was talking to him and not just telling another member of the foursome to tee off. Bounds fired, hitting Pilotto in the shoulder, and then the hit man stood up and walked out of the bushes. Pilotto, according to Bounds, fell down, held up his hands and pleaded with the shooter not to fire. But Bounds continued to blast away, firing three more shots at the mob boss. Bounds turned to leave but just missed shooting himself in the foot when the gun discharged accidentally.

Then the would-be assassin took off, forgetting to take along his knapsack which he left behind in the bushes. Running like a quick dash man, Bounds made better time than he had during the dress rehearsal. He reached the rendezvous point ahead of his wheelman Ciarrocchi.

Meanwhile, Al's foursome used golf towels on Pilotto's wounds and drove the golf cart to a nearby condominium where they phoned the hospital.

The next morning Bounds, knowing he screwed up, met both Guzzino's at the cab company. But he was not "chewed out" and spent the rest of the day driving a cab. Later Bounds got some bad news. Sam Guzzino told the would-be killer that there was suspicion in Chicago Heights that he, Bounds, was the would-be assassin. Guzzino gave Bounds some money and told him to go to Atlanta, Georgia, and lay low.

But after moving around from place to place Bounds, tired of looking over his shoulder, went to Chicago and, as we mentioned, turned himself in to Bill Lambie, the associate director of the Chicago Crime Commission.

While prosecutors were building their case against Richard Guzzino and Ciarrocchi, the 71 year old mob boss was recovering from his wounds. By the spring of 1982, Pilotto was fit enough to stand trial on labor racketeering charges in Miami. Pilotto was one of eleven men, including Chicago's top mob boss Tony Accardo, to face charges in a kickback scheme that prosecutors in Florida said milked $2,000,000 from the Laborers Union benefits funds.

Although Pilotto and seven others were convicted by the Miami Federal Jury, co-defendant Tony Accardo was acquitted. It marked the last time that the aging Chairman of the Board, as Accardo was called, would be brought to a courthouse as a defendant in criminal action. He would carry his boast to the grave that he had never spent a night in jail.

For Pilotto it was another matter. Judge James Kehoe showed no mercy to the south suburban rackets' boss when he was sentenced in September of 1982. Kehoe gave Pilotto the maximum 20 year sentence for the labor racketeering conviction. Judge Kehoe took the action following a two and a half hour sentencing hearing where an FBI agent described Pilotto as a street boss in the Chicago mob.

Another government witness said Pilotto ordered the murder of one Dino Valente because Pilotto thought the 41 year old Valente was cheating on him and losing some of his vending machine business purposely. Valente was found dying of shotgun wounds outside a restaurant in Calumet City in 1978.

It was also revealed at the hearing that the FBI had planted an agent as a doorman at a Chicago Heights nightclub. The agent was able to eavesdrop on associates of Pilotto who described Al's role in running the rackets in the south suburbs.

Also introduced at the hearing was a picture of the mob's "Politburo" taken in 1976 at the now shuttered Sicily restaurant on Chicago's northwest side. Pilotto was shown seated and grinning with other chieftains, including Tony Accardo and Joey "The Doves" Aiuppa. The exhibit was introduced to show that Pilotto was chummy with the Chicago mob's top brass.

After hearing details of Pilotto's mob activities the Judge not only handed down the maximum sentence but denied an appeal bond and ordered Pilotto to begin serving his sentence immediately.

While Pilotto began serving his time at the Federal Correctional Facility at Sandstone, Minnesota, the government indicted Richard Guzzino and Robert Ciarrocchi on charges of conspiracy, obstruction of justice, and unlawful use of a weapon.

The trial at the Dirksen Federal Building in downtown Chicago began in October, 1984, with Strike Force Attorneys Gary Shapiro and John Evon for the prosecution and the colorful Frank Oliver and Gerald Werksman representing the defendants. With Oliver on deck, the court buffs filled the courtroom of Federal Judge William Hart expecting to see quite a show. And with a mob hit man, albeit a bungler, as a key witness for the government, the buffs got their money's worth. Prosecutor Shapiro said it was one of the rare times in Chicago that a hit man had testified for the government against his mob bosses.

Bounds was the "bell cow" of the Justice Department's case and if his testimony stood up the defendants would be getting a one-way ticket to a federal pen. Oliver and Werksman attacked the credibility of Bounds, contending he was a wife beater and a scum. They described the government's star witness as a drug user and a bust-out who couldn't even hold a job as a dishwasher. The defense argued that Bounds was a liar, that he had concocted his story so that he could get into the government's witness protection program. Then ridiculing Bounds' marksmanship, the defense said the real target was Sam Guzzino and that he had shot Pilotto by mistake.

Lawyer Oliver rubbed it in even more when he belittled Bounds by saying, "He couldn't hit the broadside of a bear with a bow fiddle."

Pilotto, himself, took the witness stand for Uncle Sam testifying under a grant of immunity. He put cold water on allegations that he had planned to testify against Accardo and his co-defendants at the Miami trial in 1982. Said Pilotto, "It never entered my mind to testify about Accardo and the others." Looking hale and hearty Pilotto appeared in good spirits when he was on the stand. Perhaps, he felt a few days at the Metropolitan Correctional Center in downtown Chicago were a lot better than a cell at Sandstone where he was being held in northern Minnesota. Pilotto, who described the shooting incident on the golf course in detail, did not implicate the two defendants.

The trial of Guzzino and Ciarrocchi was winding down. In fact, the jury was beginning to deliberate when defendant Ciarrocchi suffered a heart attack. He was taken to a hospital and the presiding Judge William Hart ordered a mistrial.

A re-match was in order and the participants went through the motions again the following spring. It was the same cast of characters with the exception of prosecutor Judy Dobkin taking over for John Evon. Evon was involved in another federal case and Judge Hart wanted to resume the trial as soon as possible.

This time no one was stricken and even though Ciarrocchi contended star witness Bounds had made up the whole story, a federal court jury thought otherwise. Ciarrocchi had protested that Bounds had told a fairy story to "ruin my life," but the jury must have felt the fairy stories came from the defense side. At any rate both defendants were found guilty of one count each of conspiracy, obstruction of justice, and unlawful use of a weapon.

As for witness Bounds, he eventually became a non-person and apparently is living somewhere under an assumed

name. Defense lawyers Oliver and Werksman had a field day
attacking his character. Bounds conceded under cross examination to the regular use of drugs, including heroin, cocaine,
and marijuana. He admitted that he was a paid witness under
the government's witness protection program. But apparently
his story of the bungled assassination attempt stood up as far
as the jury was concerned.

In the

United States Court of Appeals
For the Seventh Circuit

Nos. 85-2413, 85-3099
UNITED STATES OF AMERICA,

Plaintiff-Appellee,

v.

RICHARD GUZZINO and ROBERT CIARROCCHI,

Defendants-Appellants.

Appeal from the United States District Court
for the Northern District of Illinois, Eastern Division.
No. 84 CR 304—William T. Hart, Judge.

ARGUED OCTOBER 24, 1986—DECIDED JANUARY 27, 1987

Before WOOD, JR., and POSNER, *Circuit Judges,* and
ESCHBACH, *Senior Circuit Judge.*

WOOD, JR., *Circuit Judge.* Were this attempted murder
case not so serious, a recitation of some of its facts might
suggest a Marx Brothers skit instead of a relationship to
organized crime.

On April 11, 1984, defendants Richard Guzzino and Robert
Ciarrocchi were charged with conspiracy to deprive a United
States citizen of his right to provide information and tes-
tify as a witness in a judicial proceeding, in violation of

---

*Government document denying appeal to the two men who set up
Pilotto.*

In June, 1985, Judge Hart sentenced Guzzino to 15 years
in prison while his colleague, Ciarrocchi, was given a ten year
term. An appeal attempt failed when the Seventh Circuit Court
of Appeals turned down their appeal on January 27, 1987.

Pilotto was trundled back to Sandstone but a year later he surfaced again, this time with an appearance before a U. S. Senate Committee. Grilled by the lawmakers Pilotto admitted that he often had dinner with Accardo, Aiuppa, and other syndicate leaders in Las Vegas. But Al said he didn't know what type of work his dining companions did. As Al, always the gentleman, put it, "I didn't feel like I should ask then."

Pilotto was released from prison on September 11, 1992, after 20 years behind bars. He returned to Chicago Heights where he died on January 20, 1999. Pilotto was 88 years old and had outlived his former associates Tony Accardo and Joey Aiuppa.

Attorney Carl Walsh who represented Pilotto at the trials of Guzzino and Ciarrocchi said he had no problems with his client, "Al was always a gentleman."

19

YOU GOT ME REAL GOOD

He was considered one of the mob's top hit men and by the time a nine hour interrogation was over, FBI agents Jack O'Rourke and Tom Noble had gotten an earful. When Gerald Scarpelli began telling tales out of school in 1988 he became the first Outfit torpedo to go that route.

Gerald Scarpelli told tales out of school to the FBI.

Scarpelli gave the feds a mother lode of information. He described not only the slayings he was involved in but gave agents an inside look at the mob hierarchy. He detailed the personnel and territory of each crew, including who were the honchos and who were the soldiers. He told the agents about a number of robberies and armored car jobs. And last but not least, he told how the Chicago mob collected thousands of dollars in street taxes from bookmakers and others.

True, there had been others who had traded in black hats for white fedoras, but they were in a different league than Scarpelli.

Ken Eto was involved in gambling, Frank Culotta was a lower echelon hoodlum, and Lenny Patrick was a fringe syndicate soldier who was operating independently when he gunned down rivals in the 1930s and 1940s. Daniel Bounds was a novice in his first and only try at mob stardom. The revelations of Nick Calabrese helped the government put together an indictment in the "Family Secrets" case. Whether Nick Calabrese was in the same league as Scarpelli is doubtful. Scarpelli was a feared man on the street, much more so than Nick Calabrese, who operated in the shadow of his older brother, Frank Calabrese.

Gerald Scarpelli was considered a reliable enforcer and a stand-up guy. It was unthinkable that he would ever cooperate with Uncle Sam. And when word got out on the street that he was spilling the beans, a few of the boys were shaking in their boots.

Gerald Hector Scarpelli was born in New York on January 22, 1938. The family later moved to Chicago and Jerry, as he was known to his friends, attended Austin High School where he reportedly played on the football team. Scarpelli was not a big man standing only 5' 7", but he was not diminutive either. Jerry weighed a solid 165 pounds and kept in shape lifting weights and running as much as five miles a day. He was proud of his physical condition and strongly denied he

Real

ever used any kind of drugs. In fact he told FBI agents that he was never involved in any type of narcotics activity and claimed that he didn't even use any aspirin.

Although Scarpelli claimed he was only a truck driver, he had been arrested 18 times in a career of crime that spanned almost 30 years. His arrests included charges of armed robbery, kidnapping, burglary, aggravated assault, gambling, counterfeiting, auto theft, and violation of the national firearms act. Despite his jousts with the law he was never charged with murder.

His ports of call included the Green Bay State Penitentiary in Wisconsin, the Terre Haute Federal Penitentiary in Indiana, the Oxford Federal Correctional Institution in Wisconsin, the Sheridan Correctional Center in Illinois, and the DuPage County Jail. Federal Authorities say when Scarpelli wasn't behind bars, he was a busy man toiling for his mob superiors.

But that all came to an end on July 16, 1988, when Scarpelli was taken into custody in the parking lot of a hotel in Homewood, Illinois. Scarpelli thought he was going on a burglary at a Bradley, Illinois jewelry store with his longtime buddy James "Duke" Basile. Scarpelli's girlfriend had driven him to the parking lot where Scarpelli jumped into Basile's car and transferred a gray nylon bag to the Basile vehicle.

Scarpelli didn't know it but Basile was a government informant. For two years "Duke" had worn a body recorder and whenever he met with Scarpelli his conversations were being recorded by the FBI. The Scarpelli-Basile chats included 111 transcripts of tape recorded conversations between the two men, 60 of them over the telephone and 51 in person.

In one instance, agents trying to get into Scarpelli's confidence, set up a contrived burglary in Michigan City, Indiana. The FBI rented a house in that northwest Indiana community and placed a safe in the basement. Basile told Scarpelli that the home was a summer rental of a major narcotics dealer and that a safe in the house contained a large sum of money and cocaine. When the men entered the house the G-Men caught the phony burglary on tape. Scarpelli and Basile exited the house with a quantity of government supplied cash and a small amount of coke. Scarpelli had told the government that he was never involved in drugs but apparently was not shy about grabbing some cocaine as swag.

The video tape of the phony burglary set Scarpelli back on his heels but those recorded conversations were more than frosting on the cake. In one of the conversations Scarpelli told Basile how to get rid of a body. Scarpelli suggested putting the remains in a drum filled with sulfuric acid. That way Scarpelli explained, "with sulfuric acid, in a day there won't be anything left, not even bones."

In another chat with Basile, Scarpelli described a sit down with Joe, Rocky, and Sam. The Justice Department said Scarpelli was referring to Joe Ferriola, Rocky Infelise, and Sam Carlisi, all members of the Chicago mob's hierarchy. Scarpelli told Basile on tape that if FBI agents had seen him meeting with the trio, "they all would be in the electric chair." Federal sources believe that at any confab Scarpelli had with Ferriola, Infelise, and Carlisi the subject would have had to have been about murder.

The Bureau felt it had plenty of evidence to implicate Scarpelli in a number of crimes but forcing him to surrender without bloodshed might be another matter. The agents had staked out the parking lot where Basile and Scarpelli were to link up before going on their score.

Scarpelli was not a man to be taken lightly. Ed Marshall, a Channel Two News producer, was told that when the FBI closed in on Scarpelli they didn't take any chances. Ed's sources said there were 30 armed agents including a SWAT team on the scene because the lawmen knew of Scarpelli's reputation and feared he might resort to gun play.

It turned out there wasn't any. When FBI agents approached Basile's car, Scarpelli was in the passenger seat. The surprised Scarpelli surrendered meekly. The bag Scarpelli was lugging was filled with material that a professional burglar might need. Among the items, a Sten submachine gun, a Luger pistol, and magazines filled with ammunition. In addition the lawmen found binoculars, a flashlight, a baseball cap, work gloves, and a phony nose and eyebrows. That's not the type of material that a truck driver would need on the job, since Scarpelli always contended he was just a truck driver.

On the way to the Dirksen Federal Building in downtown Chicago agents O'Rourke and Noble told Scarpelli not to ask or answer any questions, just listen. O'Rourke later testified at a hearing that he and Noble told Scarpelli about the overwhelming amount of evidence the Bureau had accumulated.

They revealed how Basile had been cooperating for two years and had been wearing a concealed body recorder and that all of the conversations between the two men had been electronically recorded and listened to by FBI agents. The meeting Scarpelli had with crime syndicate big shots had been surveilled and photographed and a Michigan City burglary Scarpelli and Basile pulled off had been surveilled, photographed, and recorded.

Then there was the matter of a northwest side garage where Scarpelli had stashed some weapons and other items in a stolen car. The FBI not only knew about the cache of weapons but itemized them as well. Among the items found in a duffel bag inside the car were a MAC 10 submachine gun, pistols, revolvers, Halloween type face masks, walkie-talkies, handcuffs, gloves, and books containing the frequencies of various law enforcement agencies.

When Scarpelli and his two companions arrived at the FBI office in the Dirksen Building O'Rourke and Noble continued to recite a litany of other incriminating evidence, but by then Scarpelli had enough. After examining some photographs Scarpelli said, "You guys are pretty slick; you got me real good."

Scarpelli was placed in an interview room on the ninth floor where he was handcuffed and seated at a chair. There according to court transcripts the suspect was advised of his rights. Asked by the two agents if he understood his rights, Scarpelli replied, "Yeah, I've been through this before." Scarpelli was then offered the opportunity to call his lawyer. Scarpelli declined, fearing word of his arrest would get out. Court transcripts show that Scarpelli was repeatedly offered coffee, soft drinks, and food. He declined those offers but was permitted to use the bathroom on several occasions.

At the beginning of the interrogation the agents laid out the evidence against Scarpelli and urged the mobster to co-operate and consider becoming a government witness. At about 11 p.m. Scarpelli decided to co-operate and signed a waiver of rights form. Then O'Rourke and Noble told Scarpelli the type of co-operation the Justice Department expected from him. The Bureau wanted Scarpelli to meet with other members of the Outfit while wearing a body recorder.

Scarpeilli reportedly agreed but said to avoid suspicion he would have to be free and under close FBI surveillance. The FBI would not buy that, and even if they did, some Justice Department officials were opposed to the idea of Scarpelli running loose even with some semblance of supervision. It became a moot point anyway, since Scarpelli never saw the light of day outside the Metropolitan Correctional Center where he was imprisoned for almost ten months.

By 3 a.m. Sunday July, 17th Scarpelli began laying it out on the line. He confessed to a variety of crimes, ranging from armed robberies to murders. At 4:45 a.m., some six and a half hours after the questioning began, agents O'Rourke and Noble had a treasure trove of information. But then the well ran dry. Scarpelli was taken over to the MCC (Metropolitan Correctional Center). Before O'Rourke and Noble could grill their prized "pupil" any further Scarpelli's lawyer put the kibosh on that. Scarpelli never volunteered any more information to the feds. Apparently he feared his chat with the FBI would prove fatal to him if his mob superiors found out. From that point on Scarpelli's lawyers tried to suppress all evidence against him on the robbery charges and his lengthy interview with the two FBI agents. Scarpelli claimed his rights were violated when he was arrested and grilled by the G-Men. It took months before a federal judge ruled on the suppression matter and the ruling went against Scarpelli. Gerald meanwhile made no attempt to bond out and opted to spend his time at the MCC hoping to get a favorable ruling from Federal Judge Milton Shadur.

While Scarpelli remained in jail, government sleuths assessed the value of the statements he made on that warm July night in 1988. Although Scarpelli's lips were sealed once he got back to the MCC, he had not been a shrinking violet when he talked to the FBI at the Dirksen Building. He was proud of his ability to lose a "tail," meaning his skill at the wheel in evading a squad car or other law enforcement vehicles. And he minced no words when he discussed several outfit slayings.

Unfortunately for Scarpelli some government documents regarding his statements were not under government seal. The media obtained some of that material, including his statements about the Dauber murder. The public was beginning to learn something about Gerald Scarpelli. Scarpelli confessed to being part of an assassination squad that killed mob hit man Bill Dauber and his wife Charlotte on a rural Will County road in July, 1980. The Dauber murder was a high profile homicide that generated heavy media coverage. Authorities had a pretty good idea who was involved in the slaying of the couple and Scarpelli's admissions confirmed their suspicions.

Dauber himself was a feared hit man whose task had been to keep the southside chop shops in line for the outfit. But word had gotten out that Dauber was cooperating with federal authorities. He was marked for death.

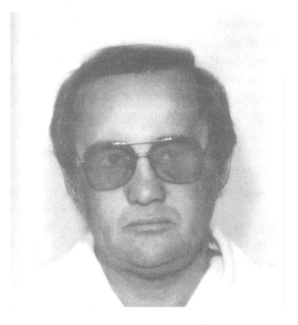

Billy Dauber—gunned down by Scarpelli and company.

In Scarpelli's own words, this is how the Dauber hit went down. "On the day of the murder I, William "Butch" Petrocelli, and Jerry Scalise were in a van. Frank Calabrese and another from his crew were in a four door Chevrolet. We drove to Joliet and waited until Billy Dauber came out of the court house. We followed Billy Dauber and his wife in their dark Lincoln towards their residence, eventually ending up on Manhattan-Monee Road in Will County."

"The car containing Frank Calabrese and the other man, who talked to us on a walkie-talkie, followed the Daubers. When the road was clear, Calabrese pulled his car in front of the Daubers and slowed down. Our van, driven by Jerry Scalise, pulled alongside the car and "Butchie" Petrocelli, using .30 caliber carbine fired out the window into the car. I also fired once with a 12 gauge shotgun. Dauber's car then swerved off the road and crashed into a big field against a tree."

Scarpelli continued his narration describing the coup de grace. Petrocelli had ordered the van to stop. "He told me to get out, telling me go make sure it's done. Finish it. I got out of the car wearing a hood or mask and walked up to the crashed car. I fired two shots from the 12 gauge shotgun into the head of Billy Dauber, hitting him." Scarpelli said he didn't fire any shots at Charlotte Dauber because she appeared dead. Scarpelli said the killers then pulled the van into a field where there were some bushes. He said Petrocelli sprayed one or two cans of lighter fluid around and set the van on fire. According to his confession Scarpelli and his confederates then got into the car driven by Frank Calabrese and fled the scene. Scarpelli said the guns were broken up and dismantled. Some of the pieces, he said were thrown into the Cal-Sag Canal.

Federal authorities said Scarpelli told Duke Basile that mob superior Joe Ferriola had sanctioned the hit on Dauber. Scarpelli told O'Rourke and Noble that at the time of the murder he did not know that Dauber was an informant. According to Scarpelli, he was told that Dauber was killed because he was not keeping the chop shops in line.

Although Scarpelli implicated his pal Jerry Scalise in the murder, Scalise was never charged in the Dauber homicide. Shortly after the Dauber murder, Scalise was arrested and convicted in London for his role in a $36,000,000 jewelry store robbery.

Petrocelli, a feared hit man, was later slain in a mob hit while Frank Calabrese was indicted in 2005 in connection with a number of murders, including the Daubers.

Scarpelli also confessed to taking part in the 1979 shotgun murder of North Chicago nightclub owner George Christofalos. He also told the agents that he helped bury mob associate Michael Oliver who was killed in a pornography store.

But Scarpelli claimed he received only "attaboys" for his work while carrying out contracts. As he explained in court documents, "It was just business." As for any salary or bonuses, Scarpelli contended he got $2,000 a month for collecting protection money from bookmakers, porno stores, and vice rings. It's no wonder that Scarpelli continued to take part in various jobs and scores to supplement his income. He admitted to taking part in two suburban armored car jobs and an Elmwood Park bank robbery, which allegedly netted Scarpelli and his partners a little over a million dollars. Undoubtedly his mob higher-ups grabbed a piece of that bank action.

Before winding up his night owl confession Scarpelli identified some of his underworld pals and described what type of criminal activities they were involved in. He also told the agents how the outfit's Chicago territory was divided and named the heads of crews that ran the various rackets in the Chicago area.

Although Scarpelli was a prime suspect in a number of gangland slayings, he would not own up to any more than the three he had mentioned. Had O'Rourke and Noble been able to continue grilling Scarpelli before his lawyers got involved, they might have even obtained more paydirt from the suburban Hillside resident.

Federal authorities don't buy the story that Scarpelli was involved in only three gangland murders. Scarpelli was a prime suspect in a rash of slayings including Police Commander Mark Thanasouras, mob enforcer Charles Nicoletti, Gerald's own pal Butch Petrocelli, aging hoodlum Ned Bakes, junkyard owner Richard Ferraro, salvage yard operator Timmy O'Brien, chop shop operator Joseph Frank Theo, car thief John Anthony Borsellino, and mob soldier Gerald Caruseillo.

Scarpelli spent more than nine months at the Metropolitan Correctional Center in downtown Chicago while his attorneys and prosecutors fought a legal battle. Justice Department lawyers wanted to use his statements he made to federal agents at the FBI office. But defense attorneys Ed Genson and Jeff Steinback argued that the statements were made under duress and should be suppressed. The government contended that Scarpelli waived his rights to remain silent while he was interrogated by agents at the Dirksen Building.

Scarpelli had been charged with robbery and conspiracy not murder or some of the other things he confessed to. But his statements to agents O'Rourke and Noble went into matters more significant than that, and those statements haunted Scarpelli. Sources told me that Scarpelli had been warned by

Jack O'Rourke—Former FBI agent who interrogated Scarpelli. Photo courtesy of Jack O'Rourke.

an inmate at the MCC to keep his trap shut or else his girlfriend and his mother would be harmed. The inmate, allegedly a mob guy from the south suburbs, was relaying a message from his superiors. At any rate Scarpelli didn't do any more talking to the government as he anxiously awaited a decision on the suppression ruling from Judge Milton Shadur. When Judge Shadur ruled that Scarpelli's statements were made of his own free will, the statements were released and were going to be made public. Scarpelli realized the game was up.

According to Assistant U. S. Attorney John Burley, Scarpelli killed himself a half hour after one of his lawyers delivered Judge Shadur's opinion. Scarpelli was found dead of apparent asphyxiation in the MCC. His body was discovered on the floor of a shower room near his cell with two plastic laundry bags drawn over his head and knotted at the throat. There were no marks on his body, which indicated there was no struggle. His death was ruled a suicide.

Why did Scarpelli kill himself? Some said he feared mob retribution while he was prison. I don't buy that. I believe Scarpelli considered himself a stand-up guy and not a stool pigeon. He did not want to spend the rest of his life being branded a squealer and a rat. So he ended it all.

Flags were not ordered to fly at half staff because of his passing. He had his share of friends, but many were very much afraid of him. Prosecutor Burley described Scarpelli this way, "He was a sociopath and a dangerous person."

As for James Duke Basile who got the goods on Scarpelli, he was released from custody. Basile faced a lengthy prison sentence but entered into a plea agreement and is now in the witness protection program where he was given a new identity. Basile, who was 69 in 2005, had also helped the Justice department in several other cases. He was living outside Chicago at last report.

20

THE OUTFIT THEN AND NOW

I couldn't believe it when I heard it—U.S Attorney General John Mitchell (later of Watergate fame) announcing in October, 1971, that the federal government had broken the back of the Chicago Crime Syndicate. I don't know what Mitchell was smoking in those days, but he was way off base with that remark. Perhaps he felt some new federal legislation was already taking its toll on organized crime, or perhaps he was trying to portray himself as a real gangbuster.

Mitchell's pronouncement was made only a year after RICO (Racketeering Influenced and Corrupt Organization) became law as part of the Organized Crime Control Act. RICO gave crime fighters some real teeth, but it took years before it had any effect on the Chicago Outfit.

I started following the Chicago Mob shortly after Sam Giancana began his involuntary exile in Mexico in the late 1960s. By the early 1970s, at the time of the Mitchell remarks, the Chicago Crime Syndicate was still in its heyday. Not only did the organization control many illicit activities in Chicago and its environs, but the Outfit, as it's called, had a big say in organized crime matters west of the Mississippi River. In fact, mob watchers have contended that organized crime families in Milwaukee, Kansas City, and San Diego were mere satellites to Chicago. Las Vegas was a Chicago fiefdom. In Los Angeles the organization there was called the "Mickey Mouse

Mafia" by Tony Accardo, while L.A. was pretty much under Chicago's thumb.

In 1982, Channel Two News spent a day at a federal courthouse in L.A. covering the trial of the top Mafiosos in the City of Angels. When court recessed in the afternoon these "leaders" of organized crime in southern California dashed out of the courthouse looking like gophers who had been flushed out of a hole in the prairie. They were trying to avoid our WBBM-TV minicam. It was not a very dignified act for men who supposedly controlled a powerful empire. Instead, these "honchos" resembled rats scurrying from a sinking ship. Certainly it was not the type of message the "brass" wanted to send to its soldiers. No wonder the Chicago gang could call the shots out west.

Back in Chicago there had been a few convictions against the boys, but it did not put much of a dent in syndicate operations. In 1970, Jack Cerone and Joe Ferriola were convicted in connection with a gambling operation. However, they were soon out of jail to become mob wheel horses again. There was also a large juice loan ring that was broken up by the FBI. However, the head of the juice loan group, Fiore "Fifi" Buccieri, was not touched. He was never even indicted.

Apparently Mitchell and his colleagues in Washington had no idea that the Outfit was skimming millions of dollars from Las Vegas casinos. The skimming operation was the mob's biggest gold mine since prohibition. That was in addition to the Outfit's normal sources of revenue—illegal gambling, juice loans, labor racketeering, extortion, and street taxes. No, the mob was alive and well in the early 1970s, but that eventually changed.

The Grim Reaper began taking its toll. The crime syndicate's chairman emeritus, Paul "The Waiter" Ricca, died of heart disease in Chicago at the age of 74. Ricca had thwarted repeated attempts by the U.S. government to deport him to Italy. He had the last laugh on Uncle Sam by succumbing in bed at Presbyterian-St. Luke's hospital in 1972. The death of Ricca, though was a blow to boss Tony Accardo, who considered Ricca one of his closest friends, a trusted colleague, and a onetime mentor.

I recall the year before when top syndicate mourners turned out for Felix Alderisio's funeral. Alderisio, known as "Milwaukee Phil," died at the age of 59 after suffering a fatal heart attack at the Marion Federal Penitentiary in southern Illinois. He had been serving a five year term for bank fraud and extortion.

Accardo and Ricca were among the Outfit elite paying their final respects at Queen of Heaven Cemetery. I watched Accardo help the ailing Ricca as the two walked out of the mausoleum to a waiting car. There was no question that Accardo held Ricca in high esteem. Accardo was the boss at that time but he relied on Ricca for advice.

Felix "Milwaukee Phil" Alderisio—There was a big turnout for his funeral. Chicago Crime Commission photo.

In a sidebar to the Alderisio funeral, one of the well dressed mourners was Joe "Joe Gags" Gagliano, described by mob watchers then as a juke box racket czar. A Channel Two News film crew and several still photographers were waiting for mob chieftains such as Gagliano to exit the affair. All of a sudden a middle aged man walked by us in his shirt sleeves, exchanging pleasantries. The reporters and photogs paid little attention to the man until he entered a car and sped away. Then it dawned on the chagrined group that Gagliano had given his coat and tie to a henchman so that he could leave the cemetery without the media recording him for posterity.

A few months after the cemetery incident, Gagliano died in his sleep in Oak Park Hospital from an apparent heart attack. He was 56 years old when he entered mob Valhalla.

Gagliano and Alderisio weren't the only Outfit big guns that had vanished from the scene. The old man with the scythe was taking a bigger toll of mob elders than the Justice Department. North side gambling boss Ross Prio of Glenview passed away in 1972. And then two high ranking mob chieftains died within a month of each other. Fiore "Fifi" Buccieri was a cancer victim in August of 1973. Then in September, Sam "Teets" Battaglia also lost the battle to the "Big C." Sam Giancana left the scene when he was murdered in his Oak Park home in 1975. But Giancana was no longer a member of the mob's ruling class since he had become a non entity when he returned from south of the border.

Despite the loss of those mob heavyweights Accardo simply filled those posts from the ranks of the "Young Turks." That meant enforcers like Joe Ferriola and Turk Torello had come to the fore. The halcyon days of the Chicago Mob would continue for a while.

A photograph confiscated by the IRS from the Lincolnwood home of Joseph "Little Caesar" DiVarco was a who's who of the Outfit. Here was the Mob's politburo sitting at a table. It was a goldmine for mob watchers as it enabled them to determine who was running the show in the mid 1970s. Wags described the gathering as the Last Supper and that's what the photograph has been called ever since.

The mobsters were meeting at an Italian restaurant on North Harlem Avenue where the boys were paying tribute to Dominic DiBella who was seriously ill and died not too long after. Since DiBella passed away in July, 1976, investigators deduce that the picture was taken in either in 1975 or 1976, shortly before DiBella died. Accardo, who was calling the shots in those days, apparently had used the DiBella affair to get his ducks in order. In other words those in attendance had been tapped for leadership positions to replace the recently departed Battaglia.

The confiscated photo of The Last Supper is shown below.

As of early 2007, the only person still alive in the group is Joey "The Clown" Lombardo, garbed in a suit with a vest. Clockwise from Lombardo is James "Turk" Torello, Joey DiVarco, "Black" Joe Amato, Accardo, Joey "The Doves" Aiuppa, DiBella, Vince Solano, Al Pilotto, and standing Jackie Cerone. Torello, mob experts said, was being groomed by Accardo to be a possible heir apparent, but he died a cancer victim at the young age of 49.

The Last Supper—Outfit bosses pay their respects to the late Dom DiBella.

The Last Supper turned out to be more than a tribute to DiBella. You could almost say it was a swan song for the Accardo apparatus because trouble from Uncle Sam was forming on the horizon.

The Las Vegas skim was still pouring money into mob coffers, and Joe Ferriola, an up-and-coming Outfit enforcer, was making sure that bookies were towing the line and paying a street tax. Mob musclemen were having no problem collecting those sky high juice loans. And some compliant unions were still under the Syndicate's domination.

The trouble that was brewing came from Washington. It came in the form of the aforementioned RICO legislation and the Omnibus Crime Control and Safe Streets Act, Title III, which authorized court approved wiretaps.

Pat Healy, the former Executive Director of the Chicago Crime Commission told me in the mid 1980s that the Outfit was very concerned that the government under RICO could seize their assets. "They are terrified of RICO. RICO does the worst thing possible. Jail terms, they can stand on their head and do a jail term, but they are terrified of RICO because it can take away all that they worked for. The government can take all their possessions, whether it's the downtown apartment, a show place home in the suburbs, or whether it's the old lady's mink coat, or their Jaguar, or Rolls Royce."

As bad as the RICO statue was for the Outfit, electronic eaves-dropping, whether a phone tap, a bug placed in an office, or worn by an informant was a real body blow.

Electronic eavesdropping played a big role in the 1982 trial of Teamsters' President Roy Williams, Outfit honcho Lombardo, millionaire insurance broker Allen Dorfman, and two others. Dorfman, prosecutors said, was the conduit between Teamster officials and organized crime. The five men were convicted in December, 1982, of trying to bribe U.S. Senator Howard Cannon, a Nevada Democrat.

The defendants conspired to bribe Cannon in a land sale in exchange for Cannon's help in killing a trucking deregulation bill. The land sale never came off and Cannon was never charged in any wrong doing. The trucking deregulation bill, by the way, did pass.

The FBI had planted two listening devices in Dorfman's insurance office and placed telephone taps on his business phones. According to government documents, agents monitored thousands of phone calls to and from Dorfman's insurance office between January 30, 1979, and June 28, 1979. At the time it was considered the most significant wiretap in FBI history. The investigation was code named Operation Pendorf (Penetrating Dorfman). And it did.

In my opinion the government would not have gotten convictions against the five defendants without the electronic eavesdropping. With the incriminating tapes played to the jury, the case was a slam dunk. It marked the first time in Federal Court in Chicago that eavesdropping devices sent major Outfit figures to jail.

RICO and the government impetus on electronic eavesdropping probably were factors in ending the Code Omerta, the oath of secrecy taken by member of the mob not to reveal syndicate secrets or inform on their peers. For years mobsters would never rat on their bosses or colleagues. In the past it was rare when a made mobster or an associate would tell tales out of school, but now the floodgates were open and a number of soldiers began spilling the beans. In some cases cooperation with the government went as far as wearing a wire and thus recording conversations with unsuspecting partners in crime.

The roll call included Ken Eto, Lenny Patrick, Frank Cullotta, James LaValley, B.J. Jahoda, and Nick Calabrese, among others. These individuals either wore recording devices and/or testified at trials against their superiors. Jahoda, for example, had a hidden video camera concealed in his apartment and often had a recording device attached to his body. Jahoda was the prosecution's big gun in a trial that sent Rocky Infelise and his crew to jail in the early 1990s.

Needless to say, with these new tools prosecutors began having a field day against the Outfit. Both bosses and mob minions began falling like ten pins. Not only that, but death and illness were making big dents in the Outfit hierarchy. A case in point—Joe Ferriola, a longtime enforcer, who had, according to many mob watchers, strong leadership skills, died in 1989 at a Houston hospital following a heart transplant operation. He was being groomed to succeed the ruling troika of Tony Accardo, Joey Aiuppa, and Jackie Cerone.

In my view the biggest blow to the ruling body since World War II was the investigation code named Operation Strawman which led to the indictment and conviction of the mob elite.

Joey "The Doves" Aiuppa—convicted in Kansas City skim case. WBBM-TV photo.

There are those who say the 2005 Family Secrets case was without doubt the strongest attempt by the Justice Department to dismantle the Chicago Outfit. I beg to differ. The 1985 Strawman trial in Kansas City sent Syndicate chieftains from Chicago, Kansas City, Milwaukee, and Cleveland to jail.

Among the defendants, who went down the tubes: Aiuppa, the day to day leader of the Chicago Outfit, underboss Jackie Cerone, near south side rackets' boss and a feared enforcer, Angelo "The Hook" LaPietra, and Joey Lombardo. That's a real big chunk of leadership being taken out of the picture. Also indicted was Tony Spilotro, the Chicago mob's boss in Las Vegas. But Spilotro was severed from the case because of illness. He was scheduled to be tried later, but that became a moot point after Spilotro and his brother, Michael, were murdered in June, 1986, as a result of a dispute between Tony and his rivals. After Tony Spilotro was eliminated, the Outfit pulled back from Las Vegas and the Buffalo crime family moved in and tried to take Chicago's place. Why Chicago abdicated there has never been fully explained.

The convictions also netted the bosses of Chicago satellites, such as Milwaukee's Frank Balistrieri, Kansas City's Carl Civella, and Milton Rockman the financial kingpin of the Cleveland Mob. Several lesser lights, including a Chicago cop and other Kansas City mobsters, also were found guilty. Nick Civella, the longtime head of the Kansas City organization died before the indictments were handed down.

The defendants were convicted of skimming more than $2,000,000 from the Stardust casino. Skimming is the practice of taking money from casino counting rooms before the cash can be counted for tax purposes, a very lucrative practice.

The trial was a marathon affair lasting over two months. The jury of six men and six women heard from 76 witnesses and listened to 33 hours of wiretaps. Some of those monitored conversations were made in the insurance office of Allen Dorfman, who was convicted in 1982 on attempted bribery charges. Many of those conversations heard in Dorfman's place of business were very germane to the Las Vegas skimming case.

The jury got the case on a Friday but did not return its guilty verdicts until Tuesday. The lengthy deliberations gave hope to the defendants that they might beat the rap. Jack Cerone told me on the courthouse steps on Tuesday morning that, "The jury is hung." Several hours later the jury came in with its guilty verdicts. Again, like the Dorfman trial, government tapes gave the prosecution a big edge.

Any doubt about the prominence of the defendants was answered when Prosecutor David Helfrey of the Justice Department's Organized Crime Strike Force in Kansas City told Judge Joseph Stevens, Jr. "There is nobody in this country who is higher in organized crime circles than (Joseph) Aiuppa."

The Kansas City trial, coupled with the 1992 death of Tony Accardo, and the convictions of Rocky Infelise and Sam Carlisi, plus the demise of Joe Ferriola, really broke the back of the Outfit some twenty years after John Mitchell's pronouncement.

Now don't get the idea that the Family Secrets' case was small potatoes. Far from that. Family Secrets, dealt with unsolved gangland murders, some eighteen in all. That was unique, something that hadn't been done before. Because we are dealing with gangland slayings here, it's a little more exciting than cases dealing with extortion, bribery, illegal gambling, and skimming money out of a casino.

But the Outfit had been severely weakened prior to Family Secrets. And the defendants in Kansas City were in a different league than those that went on trial in Chicago. Joey Lombardo was "numero uno" in Family Secrets. Lombardo was not even the "top gun" among his co-defendants in Missouri.

There is no question that the Outfit, like the "Old Grey Mare," isn't what it used to be. Authorities are divided, in their views, as to who is running the show these days. The way things are going you need a scorecard to know the players. The La Cosa Nostra crime families in other major U.S. cities have had similar problems. Yes, traditional organized crime has been hurt by the Justice Department.

However, that does not mean they have become completely impotent. As long as you have corrupt public officials and greedy businessmen, organized crime will prosper.

The mob has always been very resourceful in finding new sources of revenue. During World War II, for example, when consumers had a difficult time finding meat, the Outfit provided black market beef, although there were some who believed it was horse meat they were eating. For those who wanted more sugar, gas, and other rationed items, the mob would supply phony coupons. As one syndicate mobster said, "We deliver what the public wants."

Since 9/11, terrorism has been the main focus of the FBI and other federal law enforcement agencies. Intelligence gathering on Outfit activities has taken a back seat. The Chicago Police department's Intelligence unit has turned its main attention to street gangs who are responsible for so many crimes of violence. Thus, the Outfit won't have John Law breathing down its back as it was before. That doesn't mean the mob is getting a pass. It means they won't be under so much scrutiny.

The famous Last Supper picture, showing the mob hierarchy sitting around a table, may resemble a bunch of Rotarians or Kiwanians posing at their weekly luncheon. But the Outfit is not comprised of hail fellow well met types. Its leadership can be ruthless when its interests are threatened.

Long time companions or associates can be discarded if necessary. A good example of the mob's Realpolitik came in 1978 when a federal grand jury was looking into the deaths of five burglars who had broken into Tony Accardo's River Forest home. Among the persons appearing before that grand jury was Michael Volpe, Accardo's houseman. Five days after he went before the grand jury, the 75 year old Volpe vanished.

Federal investigators believe that Volpe was killed in order to silence him so that he could not implicate Accardo with any wrong doing. Volpe was no hoodlum, but he was expendable because he was in a position to tell the government things that the feds weren't suppose to know. As one federal agent put it back then, "They can play plenty rough when they have to." What was true then is still true today.

21

ON THE BACK BURNER

The name of the game in television, whether on a network or local level, is to make the screen "wiggle." A good newspaper story isn't always a good television story. Television news, from its infancy in the early 1950s until the present, has needed pictures to help make its point. An anchor man droning on about some tragedy has to have some kind of video to make the piece hit home. Sure, there all kinds of fonts, graphics, and gimmicks to assist in telling the story, but there is no substitute for moving video.

I remember trying to anticipate what gangland slayings would be on the Family Secrets table. Family Secrets was the code name for the big mob murders indictment that was announced in April, 2005. There had been much speculation about the case for months, so TV newsrooms wanted to have the proper video on hand to enhance the story when it finally came down.

Producer Ed Marshall, and editor Deborah Segal, and I went to the Channel Two tape archives long before the indictments were announced by the U.S. Attorney's office at the Dirksen Federal Building. We wanted to be ready to go on the air with the "right stuff" when the indictment was returned.

We ruled out the high profile murders of Sam Giancana, Dick Cain, and Charles Nicoletti. The suspects in the Giancana case were all dead. People involved in the 1973 assassination of Cain at a west side sandwich shop were either deceased or in jail. And the killers of Nicoletti were pretty much unknown, although there has been speculation that the 1977 Nicoletti murder was connected to some Milwaukee mobsters or was fallout from the 1975 Giancana slaying.

We correctly predicted that the murders of the Spilotro brothers, the slayings of Billy and Charlotte Dauber, the assassination of Danny Siefert, and the incredible demise of Michael Cagnoni would be among the murders included in the Family Secrets case. But others we thought would be a lock to be in the package were not.

One of those was the slaying of Allen Dorfman, the millionaire insurance broker. We had plenty of tape of Dorfman but as his one time co-defendant Roy Williams used to say, "Put it on the back burner." Instead of any movement on the case, it has been "put on the back burner."

Allen Dorfman—shot to death in broad daylight as he went to lunch at a suburban hotel.

The 60 year old Dorfman was gunned down on January 20, 1983, in broad daylight in the parking lot of a Lincolnwood hotel. Dorfman and his companion, Irv Weiner, were going into the hotel for lunch after stopping at a video store to pick up a copy of the movie *The Verdict*. The killers made sure their deadly mission was a success. The killers shot the perpetually tanned and elegantly dressed Dorfman eight times at point blank range. As in the slaying of Sam Giancana, the murder weapon was a .22 caliber pistol. Weiner was not injured in the fusillade and was either unwilling or unable to help detectives identity the killers who wore masks.

Investigators came to the conclusion that Dorfman had become a liability. He was facing a lengthy prison term from his conviction in the Senator Cannon attempted bribery case. And only days before, he was indicted in San Francisco in connection with an alleged kickback scheme involving two union locals in California.

Authorities theorize that Outfit higher ups felt that Dorfman, unwilling to spend the rest of his life in prison, would be willing to cooperate and spill mob secrets. If so, he could take down some of his mob colleagues. Detectives believed that the mob brass felt that Dorfman would talk to get a soft sentence or even enter the witness protection program.

Obviously a hit on Dorfman had to be approved by someone like Joey Aiuppa or Tony Accardo. But the intriguing question, who actually killed Dorfman, has not been answered.

Investigators did regard one Ray Spencer as a pretty good suspect. But the 44 year old Spencer was found dead in his Florida apartment in 1984, a year and a half after Dorfman was slain. Several Justice Department officials told me they definitely thought Spencer was involved.

Spencer, a lower echelon crime syndicate figure was seen in the Lincolnwood area the morning of the murder. Spencer was a big guy, around six foot one and weighing more than 250 pounds. He matched the description of one of the assassins and he also lived in the area where the murder weapon was found. But Spencer did not have a reputation of doing any heavy work (contract killing).

After Spencer's name surfaced in the investigation, a relative of the suspect called Channel Two and said there was no way that Ray was the killer. The relative claimed Spencer could not have fled the crime scene, as described by witnesses, because of his girth. The relative said that Spencer could hardly walk, let alone run. Spencer was never charged with the Dorfman slaying and, for that matter, neither was anyone else.

Prior to the Family Secrets indictment we also pulled out old film and video tape of Charles "Chuckie" English. However, like the Dorfman murder, we didn't need it.

English, a onetime high ranking crime syndicate boss, was shot to death in the parking lot of an Elmwood Park restaurant. The 70 year old English had just dined on roast pig at the now shuttered Horwath's restaurant when he was assassinated on St. Valentine's Day eve in 1985. Among English's dining companions at a large table of 12 were two Cook County Judges and two Elmwood Park Village Trustees.

The killers, two men wearing ski masks, were waiting for English to exit the restaurant and as he approached his parked Cadillac, they let him have it.

English, described in his heyday as a juke box czar like the late Joe Gagliano, was a confederate of Sam Giancana. When Giancana appeared before a federal grand jury in downtown Chicago in 1974, it was English who drove the onetime mob boss home. English lost his clout when his mentor was murdered in his Oak Park home a year later. Chuck's star with the Outfit began to sink.

In the fall of 1981, a Channel Two News undercover unit spotted English hanging out at a west side service station which was a drop off point for mob bookies. The gas station was frequented on a daily basis by crime syndicate gambling figures. But at that point, investigators said, English's role had been relegated to that of a gofer. He may have been trying to get back into the action in1985 when he stepped on somebody's toes and was killed.

Charles "Chuckie" English—slain in a parking lot after dining on roast pig. Chicago Crime Commission photo.

I would have bet the mortgage that the murder of Patrick "Patsy" Ricciardi would have been in the Family Secrets umbrella, but it wasn't. Ricciardi, a colorful character and a gaudy dresser, ran the Admiral Theater on the city's northwest side. The Admiral wasn't just another neighborhood movie house because for seven days a week it ran hard core pornographic films. Spliced in between these flicks, the Admiral featured live entertainment, exotic dancers who would titillate the house clientele already aroused from the gyrations seen on the silver screen.

The Admiral was a moneymaker, no doubt about that. Ricciardi had taken a closed movie house and turned it into a cash cow. Ricciardi always denied any mob connections but he was a cousin of the late "Milwaukee Phil" Alderisio, a convicted mob enforcer and extortionist. That relationship to "Milwaukee Phil" didn't hurt him in certain circles.

Ricciardi was last seen alive by the theater manager on a July morning in 1985. He told his underling that he had a business appointment. Detectives believe that appointment was with Patsy's killer. Two days later, on July 25th,, the body of the 59 year old Ricciardi was found in the trunk of a stolen car. He had been shot once in the head.

Why was Ricciardi slain? Authorities would not confirm it but street talk had it that he was informing on the mob and the boys didn't like it. Another theory was that he was cheating on people who really owned the Admiral Theater. In other words, some contended "Patsy" was only a front and not the real boss of the Admiral.

One of the suspects in the murder was a defendant in the Family Secrets case. But as of this writing no one has been charged with Ricciardi's homicide. Ironically, Ricciardi's death occurred during the same week that a Federal Commission on pornography held hearings in Chicago.

In preparing for the Family Secrets story we had a strong suspicion that the murder of chop shop operator Timmy O'Brien would also be a part of the hit parade. We knew that federal authorities connected to the Family Secrets case were questioning some people about the killing, but the O'Brien homicide is still gathering dust.

Timmy O'Brien was an Oak Lawn resident, about 40 years old, who ran two auto repair yards in the southern suburbs. Sheriffs Police said the yards were fronts for the stolen parts racket. In other words, detectives said, O'Brien was in the business of chopping up stolen luxury cars and selling the parts, which is known in the trade as the chop shop racket. The racket apparently was very lucrative.

The way we heard it was that O'Brien was getting fed up with paying the Outfit a tribute in order to stay in business. Reportedly about two months before he was killed mobsters told him that they were jacking up the monthly street tax. He balked at that.

In April, 1979, underworld gossip had it that a contract had been put out on O'Brien's life. O'Brien though boasted to one detective that he was an "Irish Mafioso" and would stand up to the Outfit. The media became aware of O'Brien's problems and were not surprised when he was AWOL for a court appearance. His lawyer, at that time, told the judge "He (O'Brien) is missing and presumed dead."

Indeed he was. In June, 1979, O'Brien's body, riddled with shotgun pellets, was found in the trunk of a car in Blue Island. Although investigators had several ideas as to the killers' identity, nobody was ever charged in the case. One of the principal suspects is dead. The case is still open but the chances of it being solved are getting more remote.

Before bailing out, there is one old case we want to touch base with, albeit briefly. It had nothing to do with Family Secrets and got little media coverage. It's one that armchair sleuths can try their deductive powers in solving, something detectives haven't been able to do.

We are referring to the execution style murder of four Park Ridge businessmen in July, 1977, which continues to puzzle "Hawkshaws," both of the amateur and professional variety. The four men were found shot to death, stacked into piles, in an elevator of a Park Ridge office building. There was no evidence of any robbery; it was strictly an execution. The murder weapon was a mob favorite, a .22 caliber semi-automatic.

The victims were all involved in a firm that sold items such as fire and burglar alarms. The men were described as high rollers, whose lifestyle and business practices may have angered the wrong people. Police have believed that the financial dealings of the four men were the motive for the assassination. The slaying caught the attention of the media for several days, but now the case is as cold as a mackerel.

22

DOWN MEMORY LANE

People often ask, what is the most interesting story you ever covered? Of course there are so many of them, it's hard to pinpoint just one or two. I think that some of the events that occurred in the late 1960s and 1970s in Chicago left an indelible impression.

That was when the city was rocked by the riots following Dr. Martin Luther King's death and the disturbances surrounding the 1968 Democratic National Convention in Chicago. I'll never forget looking out of the window in the Wrigley building (I was working at WIND then) toward the west side in April, 1968, and seeing huge clouds of smoke. The scene resembled a German city that had been bombed by the RAF during World War II. It was unbelievable. Driving home on North Lake Shore Drive on Saturday morning after work, around 2 a.m., was strange. I encountered one other car, that's all. Normally on a Friday night, even at that hour, there would be a fair amount of traffic on the Drive. People were so concerned about the west side rioting that they weren't venturing out from their homes. It was an eerie feeling going north on the Drive and not seeing anybody.

The August mayhem during the convention was something else. I recall running to get out of the way when Chicago Police, riot gear and truncheons in hand, began one of their famous sweeps. I didn't get hit, but some media members and demonstrators as well as onlookers got clobbered. Word on the street had it that police had told local reporters to wear a suit or sport coat so they wouldn't look like hippies, or otherwise expect a date with a billyclub.

In justice to the police, the demonstrators did all they could to provoke them. Many of the protestors wanted a bloody confrontation so it would give the impression to a world wide audience that the authorities were nothing more than bloody fascists.

The demonstrators would toss chunks of excrement at the cops while chanting obscenities to the men in blue. The police had to stand under a hot August sun while the protestors made remarks about the cop's ancestors being of the four legged variety or even worse. Police personnel are supposed to be highly disciplined and immune to verbal abuse from the citizenry, but they are human too. There is no question that some overreacted. Much of the violence was captured on live television as viewers saw a steady diet of cops battering young demonstrators. Unfortunately television did not show what often provoked the police. At any rate the city got quite a black eye from that turbulent week, and the police department had to take its share of the blame.

The violence and street protests didn't end with the convention. Peace demonstrations against the Vietnam War were the norm every weekend. There were disturbances in Chicago public high schools, many not connected to the peace movement.

And then came the "Days of Rage" in the fall of 1969 when young radicals went on a rampage along the Gold Coast and in the Loop. College campuses were erupting and even at Northwestern University, not exactly known as a hotbed for radicals, student protestors barricaded Sheridan Road in Evanston.

It was quite a time to be a reporter in Chicago. It was something you can't forget. It sounds farfetched now, but for

Mob under boss, Jack Cerone as he arrives for trial in Kansas City. WBBM-TV photo.

a time I thought that the city was going up for grabs. Fortunately there were assignments that dealt with subjects other than demonstrations and street rumbles.

I always enjoyed doing stories about the Chicago Outfit. They were most always good yarns and the public seemed to be fascinated hearing tales about gangsters. I wish I could have interviewed the late mob boss Tony Accardo, but he didn't talk to reporters. Mob underboss Jack Cerone was a very articulate guy who would stop for a chat. However, he would never do it in front of a camera.

One of the things I enjoyed most was the "Chicago Chronicles" series that ran three times a week on the 6 p.m. news. The show had a shelf life of two years before a new management team put the kibosh on the Chronicles. I was given pretty much of a free hand in selecting what personalities I wanted to cover. Those subjects, I guess you could say, were a lot of Damon Runyon characters. They ran the gamut from prize fighters, pro grapplers, cabbies, bartenders, newsies, mobsters, bookies, strippers, and hash slingers, to Joe and Sally Sixpack. As we said about our subjects when we signed off each piece, "You won't read about them in the Chicago guide books or travel brochures."

We don't have the space to list the many interviews we found interesting. There were a number of "one on ones" with Presidents, including Richard Nixon and Ronald Reagan. However, one interview that really stood out as fascinating was a lengthy chat with a notorious gangster, a member of Tony Spilotro's "Hole In The One" gang, Lawrence "Big Foot" Neumann.

Neumann wasn't a typical underworld character. He had no reason to turn to a life in crime. He came from a well-to-do family and had a steady income from a trust fund established by his father. But, he went into wrong doing in a big way. He had an explosive temper and as a young man killed three persons in an Uptown bar because he felt he had been short changed.

We interviewed Neumann in 1984 at the Metropolitan Correctional Center in Chicago where he was being held on federal firearms charges. He was a powerfully built man with huge hands. It was obvious he could intimidate people with ease. At the time of the interview he was also facing state charges in the torture murder of a Chicago jeweler.

Larry was one of the most articulate news figures that I ever interviewed. There was no question he could have been a success in most fields had he so desired to go straight. Apparently the thrill of matching wits with the authorities was a challenge he could not resist.

Although he admitted to his share of wrong doing, he strongly denied that he had stabbed and strangled the jeweler Robert Brown in 1979. The jury didn't see it that way and Neumann was convicted and sentenced to a life behind bars.

Neumann died in January, 2007, at the Menard Correctional Center in southern Illinois, apparently from heart disease. Neumann, who was 79, was penniless when he perished and the state paid to cremate him.

Sports stars usually aren't the best interviews. In fact most of those head cuts you hear on radio or see on TV are boring. There are exceptions. Former light heavyweight boxing champion Archie Moore gave me one of the best interviews I had with a sports figure when he appeared on the "For The Record" show on WIND. Moore had little formal education, but because of his travels as a globe trotting boxer he was almost a citizen of the world. He was a delight to interview, and could really spellbind you when the mike was on.

The late wresting promoter Bob Luce was interesting, too—to say the word "colorful" is an understatement. So, too, was Jack Pfeifer, a pro wrestling manager of the old school, a real drum beater. The Swedish Angel was one of his grapplers.

When he was in a good mood Woody Hayes was a great interview, but, if things weren't going right, watch out. Vince Lombardi was a tough interview and he was never comfortable with the media. I enjoyed talking to former heavyweight champion Rocky Marciano. He was soft spoken but if you could draw him out, he had things to say. When I interviewed Mike Ditka, shortly after his rookie season, I felt he was going places, not only on the gridiron, but as a motivator. It was obvious he was the type of guy who could sell merchandise, which he does in countless television commercials.

One of the most considerate sports icons I interviewed was Jack Nicklaus. On two occasions, he took time out for a TV interview when he had a lot on his plate. Trying to interview his long time rival, Arnold Palmer, was a different story. In 1963, Palmer was playing an exhibition match at the Freeport, Illinois Country Club. There was a luncheon in the clubhouse before the round and when Arnie arrived, you would

*Mike Ditka interview with Drummond at Bears' training camp. 1963
WREX-TV phpto.*

have thought that the President was on the premises. Everyone in the room stood up and there was prolonged applause.
We went though his agent and asked if we could have a brief
interview with Palmer. The answer at first was no. We were
persistent enough to keep trying. Finally we were allowed to
talk to Palmer, but it was like pulling teeth before we sat down
with the former U.S. Open Champion.

Politicians usually make good interviews. Some though
have a tendency to get long winded and take off with a canned
speech. Those kinds of pols won't directly answer your question. They will beat around the bush hoping the interviewer
won't notice that the elected official's yakking has completely
skirted the issue. Some politicians see no difference between
reporters and porters. These office holders think reporters
should carry whatever baggage is handed them. Then there
are those types of public figures who are a delight to talk to.
The late Congressman Roland Libonati and Chicago pol Lou

Farina were in that league. Even if they would toe dance around the question, the interview would always be fun.

Sometimes though things don't work out the way you wanted. I had a show in primetime on WHO-TV in Des Moines called "Profile." Each week we would have as a guest a personality from the political, entertainment, or athletic world. Normally there were no problems with our guests who had been interviewed eons of times by the media. But not everything goes like clock work. "Profile" lasted a half an hour, which meant that our guest would have to expound a bit and not answer with a brief yes or no. On one occasion our guest was Art Arfons, who had recently set a land speed record at the Utah salt flats. Art may have been hell on wheels but he answered everything with a brief word or two. We tried everything, discussing drag racing, Indy cars, stock cars, his vehicle "The Green Monster," and even the weather in Salt Lake City, but to no avail. Our viewers didn't need any sleeping pills before hitting the hay that night.

Our show involving George Jessel was something else. Jessel was considered the "King of Toastmasters" and had a real gift of gab. On paper our appointment with Jessel was going to be a delight. After all George was always in demand as an after dinner speaker or toastmaster. He was a frequent guest on television talk shows and hobnobbed with the Hollywood crowd. The only trouble was that when George arrived at the WHO-TV studios for taping he was "three sheets to the wind." Not only that, but he was garbed in some kind of military uniform that made him appear to be a Banana Republic dictator of a bygone era.

The director of the show was ready to toss in the towel. He felt Jessel was in no shape to go on. Since we didn't have another show in the can I felt we had little choice but to give it a shot. And we did. Although it was obvious to the viewer that Jessel had been imbibing, he was a professional and once the camera's red eye came on George got on a roll. It turned out to be an entertaining evening.

Toastmaster Deluxe George Jessel, in some kind of unifoirm, chats with Drummond. 1966 WHO-TV photo.

As we noted in our earlier book, *Thirty Years In The Trenches,* the news business has changed tremendously from a technological standpoint, yet many things are still the same. As any television or radio personality can attest, he or she must get "good numbers" or it's out the front door. There are not as many opportunities in radio news today as there were when I started in the 1950s. However, TV newsroom opportunities are much greater. In the 1950s and even well into the 1960s, many TV stations had only a fifteen minute newscast. Contrast that with the present when news formats are on twenty fours a day. In this era young broadcasters can find themselves at a network of some kind (CNN, ESPN, FOX NEWS, MSNBC, etc.) with limited experience. The days of toiling in broadcast's minor league or tank towns for years is no longer the case. So for those aspiring journalists who want to give the news business a try, I say come on in, the water is fine.